Lost Houses of York
and the North Riding

EDWARD WATERSON
& PETER MEADOWS

Foreword by Giles Worsley

JILL RAINES
1998

See P. 34

FOREWORD

Of all the counties of England, the North Riding of Yorkshire has probably suffered among the least from the rash of country house demolitions that disfigured the countryside during this century, and particularly since the Second World War. But the number of houses illustrated in this book lost in this century is a mark of the scale of that disaster.

In many ways the North Riding was lucky. It could even be said to have benefitted from problems elsewhere as landowners retreated to its rural safety: the Mexboroughs moving to Arden Hall from Methley Hall near Leeds, the Sheffields leaving Normanby Hall near Scunthorpe for Sutton Hall, the Hills buying Clifton Castle after leaving Ireland, the Downes settling finally at Wykeham having left Cowick Hall near Goole in the 19th century and Dingley Hall in Northamptonshire in the 20th. There was no greedy metropolis like London spreading its suburban tentacles between the wars, and the only centre of industry was Middlesborough on the periphery of the county. The North Riding was, and to a remarkable extent still is, a county of substantial estates with generally good land. And yet houses of the stature of Hornby Castle, one of the country's great late medieval fortified manor houses with alterations by John Carr and perhaps by "Athenian" Stuart could be demolished, largely because of the value of its building materials. Thirkleby Hall was as perfect a Wyatt house as was ever erected but it went unlamented. Rounton Grange was among the most remarkable houses to be built in England in the late 19th century, but it lives on only in the photographs of *Country Life.*

Demolition is no new phenomenon as Peter Meadows and Edward Waterson show. It would be fascinating to know what the Percy's great medieval house at Topcliffe was like, or the Eure's Tudor mansion at Malton, demolished by two squabbling heiresses, leaving only the gatehouse, a substantial house in its own right. So far no views have come to light, and that is the North Riding's tragedy. What would we give for a well-illustrated county history like Plot's *Staffordshire* of 1686 or Chauncey's *Hertfordshire* of 1700? Luckily there is Samuel Buck's sketchbook with its mixture of large-scale drawings and thumb-nail sketches. Without it the authors' task would have been much more difficult. But even a quick analysis of Buck shows how much he did not cover. A list of contemporary houses still standing or which were illustrated by other artists is almost as long as the list of houses Buck visited. It is surprising how many even quite substantial houses listed in the mid-17th-century hearth tax returns have disappeared without trace.

Any project like this book must be a frustrating one. Given the number of houses that are only known from a single illustration or even a single reference, how many more are there that have been completely forgotten? But the work is vital. The study of country houses is too easily dictated by the accidents of survival, but the resulting history is distorted. The pages of *Country Life* form the most detailed study available for an enormous number of country houses, but it is inevitably the houses that are still lived in that are written about. Books like this one are needed to redress the imbalance. The painstaking work of finding how many houses have gone, when and why, who built them and what they looked like is essential if we are to build up a true picture of the history of the county.

The gaps in our knowledge are still large. The history of the country house in this century has still to be written. No one has yet analysed why it was that some houses were demolished and others survived. How much can be blamed on tax or the agricultural depression? How much on families failing to produce heirs? How much on loss of will and nerve? A proper list like this of the houses that have gone is the cornerstone of such a study. If we are lucky the authors will go on to do a similar study of the West Riding where the scale of the problem is even greater.

Giles Worsley
Architectural Editor
Country Life

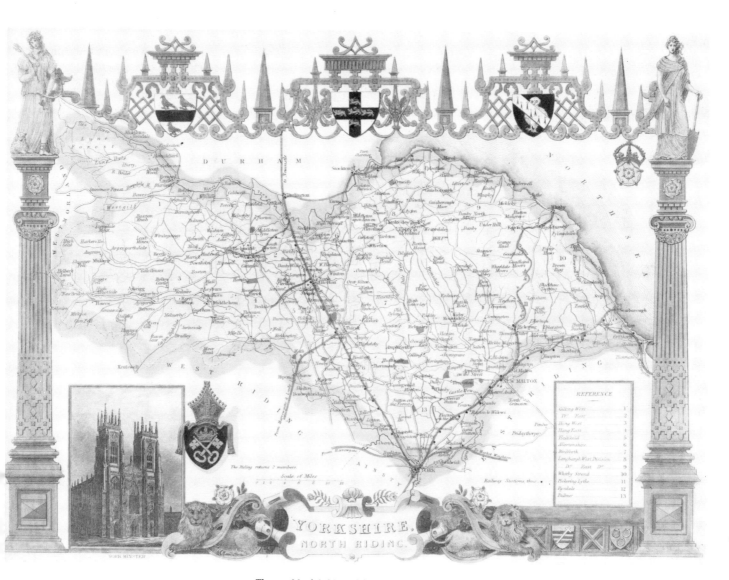

Thomas Moule's Map of the North Riding, 1840's

INTRODUCTION

This book covers the area of the North Riding of Yorkshire and the City of York as they existed until 1974. To have covered the new county of North Yorkshire would have meant including large areas of the old West Riding around Ripon and Harrogate, and south of York, and excluding areas now part of Cleveland and County Durham. Much of the topographical and architectural literature relates to the old North Riding; and there is still a sense of 'Yorkshire' in the areas which have now passed under different administrations.

More than sixty lost houses have been identified for which illustrations were available. Others disappeared before a record of them could be made. These sixty houses were widely spread through the area. There were inevitably concentrations where population and industrial expansion was greatest, around York, and in Cleveland; but it is a sad fact that many of the houses stood in or near small communities. The usual reasons for demolition apply in the North Riding: destruction by fire; the sale and break-up of the estates which supported the houses financially; the increasing costs of upkeep and repair, and the difficulty of securing adequate domestic help, in the 20th century; damage to property and the dislocation of family life caused by requisition in the two wars of this century; the loss of heirs in wartime, the burden of death duties, and the pressure to dispose of a house when a family had two or more estates.

The catalogue of notable houses sold this century for their scrap value, the architectural and ornamental features being auctioned and carried off to other houses and museums, is depressing. Stanwick Park in 1923, Sedbury Park in 1927, Hornby Castle in 1930, Halnaby Hall in 1950, Kirkleatham Hall in 1954, Sand Hutton Hall in 1955, and Wiganthorpe Hall in 1955: these were all 18th century houses with fine interiors. It is small consolation that a room from Stanwick can be visited in Minneapolis, that the front portal of Hornby Castle can be crossed in the Burrell Collection in Glasgow, that dinner can be taken in the Halnaby dining room at the Bridge Inn, Walshford, or that the authors have walked through a Thornton-le-Street door case at Upsall Castle. If these houses had survived into the age of statutory listing, they would in all likelihood have survived.

Nevertheless, these sixty houses represent a small fraction of the total number of great houses in the North Riding. Most parishes had a great house; and a glance at Pevsner's *Buildings of England* volume will show that many are still standing. A fair number of large estates survive in family hands; the Howards at Castle Howard, the Zetlands at Aske Hall, the Normanbys at Mulgrave Castle, and the Worsleys at Hovingham Hall, to name only a few. Some houses which came close to being lost have been saved, restored or rebuilt: Duncombe Park, Bolton Hall, Hackness Hall, and Castle Howard itself, after fires; Kiplin Hall and Lartington Hall after neglect or insensitive subdivision. Some great houses have been split up into smaller units, notably Brough Hall; some have found institutional use or are hotels. Yet a great many, particularly the smaller, more manageable houses, are still family homes and find willing buyers when they appear on the market.

For many counties, illustrations of houses before the advent of photography in the mid-19th century are scarce. There may be a print, perhaps, in the collections of *Seats* issued by Angus, Neale, Jones and others; or a painting by one of the topographical artists; or an elevation in *Vitruvius Britannicus* or one of the other architects' publications; or a panoramic view of house and estate in Knyff and Kip's *Britannia illustrata*. Historians of Yorkshire houses are especially fortunate in possessing the sketchbook of Samuel Buck (1696-1779), c.1720, in the British Library, reproduced in facsimile in 1979. Buck sketched over two hundred Yorkshire houses in preparation for a publication proposed by the antiquary John Warburton. A few of Buck sketches are of houses still familiar today, but the vast majority show 16th and 17th century houses long since demolished or remodelled. Most of Buck's houses survive, but in forms quite unrecognisable by him. For some houses, such as Thornton Hall, Stainsby Hall and Gilling Wood Hall, Buck is the only known source of illustration. For others, such as Stanwick Park, Hornby Castle and Hutton Bonville Hall, Buck provides an additional glimpse of the transition of these houses. For Sedbury Park and Linthorpe Hall, Buck shows that houses photographed in the 19th century had formed their distinctive appearance nearly two hundred years previously.

Some houses can be illustrated by paintings and prints as well as by Buck's sketches. Clints Hall (demolished 1843) is an example. Not many topographical paintings are as dramatic as the 'Hutton Bonville dog' of c.1725, where the monstrously large hound ranges in the foreground and the house, people and parish form the backdrop. Later in the century George Cuitt painted several North Riding houses.

Most of the lost houses reached the photographic period, and were photographed. The earliest photographs in this book, of Marton Hall and Gunnergate Hall, must date from c.1860, since both houses were transformed in following years. Interior photographs are, naturally, scarcer than exteriors: privacy, and the need for special lighting, made such views less popular and easy. We are fortunate that *Country Life* magazine recorded Halnaby Hall, Rounton Grange and parts of Hornby Castle when they were still occupied by their owners. Very often the first interior pictures were taken when the rooms were bare and the auctioneers were set to move in (if vandals had not beaten them to it).

As to architects, very little is known about the designers of the 17th century houses drawn by Buck. Robert Smithson's Slingsby Castle is a notable exception. For the 18th century, documentary evidence is usually better, and more should be known; but the architects and craftsmen employed at Sedbury Park, Halnaby Hall, Stanwick Park, Thornton-le-Street Hall and Stillington Hall are not definitely known. The list of 'suspects' at Stanwick Park is tantalising: Lord Burlington, William Kent, Sir Thomas Robinson and Daniel Garrett have all been suggested. John Carr, the major Yorkshire architect of the late 18th century, worked at Hornby Castle, Kirkleatham Hall, Upleatham Hall, Sedbury Park, Clints Hall, Sand Hutton

Hall and Wiganthorpe. James Wyatt was responsible for Thirkleby Park, Thomas Atkinson possibly for Sion Hill and Easthorpe Hall. Sir Robert Smirke made large additions to Upleatham Hall; Anthony Salvin designed Cowesby Hall and added to Sand Hutton Hall: Ignatius Bonomi designed Newton House and Clervaux Castle, and his nephew George Goldie designed Upsall Castle. Philip Webb was responsible for Rounton Grange.

York presented particular problems. It was included with the North Riding because it can be argued that in architectural and other ways it had more in common with that Riding than with the East or West. York was a regional centre and focus for the gentry of the North Riding in a way that Northallerton, the administrative town, was not. The gentry of the North Riding created many of York's finest Georgian houses. Such families as the Garforths and the Fairfaxes had town houses in York which survive, although Fairfax House came close to demolition and an entry in this book. Some significant houses changed to commercial uses, such as the Queen's Hotel, and therefore cannot be included. Many of the older houses have been recorded in Darrell Buttery's *Vanished buildings of York*.

The buildings featured here are mostly not the gentry town houses but rather the villas and semi-rural retreats which sprang up in suburban York in the late 18th and early 19th centuries. A comparison of 19th century Ordnance Survey maps with the latest edition will show how many there were, and how many have gone unrecorded. They were the houses of successful York businessmen such as James Barber, and they were

modest in scale compared with the large mansions erected by industrial magnates in Cleveland. The city was unhealthy, tracts of land could be obtained cheaply in the newly enclosed environs of York, and fashion hastened the movement. The houses were not generally of outstanding architectural merit. Yet they were often of manageable size, making their loss all the more regrettable. The fashionable air which numerous villas imparted to Heworth, for example, was their eventual undoing, since it attracted suburban estate housing in the 20th century, loss of the feeling of rural isolation which attracted the original owners, and pressure to release large grounds for further suburban housing. The houses which could not find institutional use or be subdivided were demolished.

The rules which have governed inclusion of houses in this book are as follows. Medieval castles have been excluded. Houses demolished before 1900 and not rebuilt on the same site have been included, as have houses lost since 1900, even if a new house was erected on the site. It is hoped that the present owners of Sedbury Park, Hornby Castle, Cowesby Hall, Upsall Castle, Sion Hill and Foston Hall will forgive the description of their homes as 'lost'. The rules dictate otherwise!

The descriptions are mostly too brief to be full accounts of the houses here illustrated. The authors will be grateful to receive additional information about the houses shown in this book, and other lost houses unknown to them. New sources of illustrations will be particularly welcome, as will news of the whereabouts of architectural drawings and sale catalogues.

STILLINGTON HALL

When Stillington Hall was demolished in 1966 Yorkshire lost one of its most intriguing houses whose lavish interior provided a stark contrast to its conservative exterior.

Christopher Croft (later Sir Christopher), Lord Mayor of York, bought the Stillington Estate in 1649 and it remained in the family until 1895, funded by the port shipping enterprise which bears their name. It seems likely that Christopher built a new house on the site, and later alterations incorporated a late 17th century staircase which may have come from this house.

Stephen Croft (1712-1798) inherited the estate from his namesake at the age of twenty-one and later rebuilt the house in the Palladian style. It was a brick house of seven bays and two and a half storeys, with a three-bay pediment. Under this pediment, at first floor level, the three central windows were internally only pointed lunettes in the coving to the two-storey entrance hall, surrounding a central hexagonal plaster panel. Here, as elsewhere in the house, the richness of the plasterwork, the fireplaces and the carving was surprising. Equally surprising was the low height of some of the ceilings. The Drawing Room, for instance, could not be faulted in terms of quality but its proportions were less than perfect.

In 1853, two generations later, the estate passed to Henry Croft, who met an untimely death by drowning at Balaclava the following year. His younger brother, Captain Stephen, wasted little time in improving his unexpected inheritance. Between about 1855 and 1859 he rendered the exterior and added a large three-bay Italianate porch. A new conservatory, in a similar style, appeared to the east. Internally the staircase hall, with its 17th century flights, was modified and it has been suggested that some of the apparently Palladian plasterwork dates from this time.

Next to inherit in 1871 was Harry Croft, the last of the family to live at the hall. In 1888 the whole estate was offered for sale by auction. Lot 4 was Stillington Hall and 662 acres; the successful purchaser was given "the option of purchasing at a valuation the greater part of the furniture in the mansion". There was no bid. In 1895 Harry was more successful in his efforts and agreed a sale to Mr. Rawdon Thornton, who sold to Mr. Matthew Liddell in 1903. In the 1930's the house slipped into institutional use as a home for the elderly. Later it became a Catholic school but had a lingering vandalized end. Some consolation may be derived from the salvaging of many of the interior fittings.

(1) View from south east (Victoria County History)

(2) Entrance Hall (RCHM England)

(5) The Library (D. Batty)

(3) Entrance Hall ceiling (RCHM England)

(4) The Drawing Room (D. Batty)

7

HUBY HALL

What now masquerades as Huby Hall is only a fragment of a much larger mid-17th century brick house which stood in Gracious Street, so named by its inhabitants who survived the plague. The surviving wing sports large pilasters in brick and a Dutch gable, reduced within living memory.

Its main claim to fame was that in 1720 William Radcliffe, Thomas Marshall and others sold the messuage and land to William Wakefield, the Vanbrughian amateur architect.

As early as 1852 Thomas Gill referred to the "antique ruins of Huby Hall". Today it is a modest cottage.

Huby Hall 1990

FOSTON HALL

A house has stood on this site since medieval times and the rebuilding of 1823 for the Rev. Francis Simpson probably incorporated parts of an older building. It was later sold to a Mr. Crawshaw, who sold it in 1856 to Miss Haigh (later Lady Lechmere) the young heiress to the adjoining Whitwell estate.

Alterations in 1859 included an ungainly new entrance front to the east. It reached its greatest extent when brewer Col. Tetley added a new wing in 1936. In 1958 the whole of the main block, with the exception of the two western bays, was demolished.

South Front (I. Ware)

HAXBY HALL

Haxby Hall stood at the eastern end of the village street, closing a rural vista. Originally built about 1790, it was remodelled for J. T. Tuite about 1827, at which time the semi-circular portico and balustrade were added. The central block was of two and a half storeys, flanked by two-storey wings. A long range of stables, a cottage and other outbuildings stretched to the south. The garden front presented a mixture of styles, but the eye was caught by an extraordinary piece of building design which incorporated a glass cupola over the stairwell. The park, with fishpond, extended to 22 acres.

Nineteenth century owners included various well known local names. Between the wars it was purchased by Mr. Kenneth Ward who moved out during requisitioning, which it survived without apparent mishap. He moved back when peace came but by the time he sold in 1950, housing development and playing fields had reduced the grounds to about three acres. Further land was sold off and the hall was converted into flats.

The quiet village became a dormitory for York and a roundabout was constructed outside the front door. Eventually, in about 1960, the County Council bought it and claimed to have discovered dry rot, death watch beetle and other perils. They demolished it shortly afterwards, building a fire station on the site and an old people's home which carries the name of its forebear. Apart from a few railings, no trace remains.

(1) West Front 1950 (L. Fotheringham)

(2) East Front 1950 (L. Fotheringham)

SAND HUTTON HALL

John Carr of York designed a house for William Read in 1786. It was of two storeys in white brick. A large projecting bay overlooked 100 acres of rolling parkland. This house later became the south wing of the hall, albeit disguised by later embellishments.

When William Read died in 1800 he left the Sand Hutton estate to his relative, the Rev. Thomas Cutler Rudston, whose family lived at Hayton Hall, East Yorkshire (dem. 1805). In accordance with the will, he assumed the additional surname of Read. Following Rudston-Read's death in 1838 his representatives sold the estate to James Walker of Springhead and Beverley. The Walkers' prosperity can be traced back to his great-grandfather, also James, who had flourished as a Manchester merchant in the first half of the 18th century.

James of Sand Hutton was created a baronet in 1868 and in the 1870's his estates in four counties totalled nearly 7000 acres. In 1839-41 Anthony Salvin was engaged to extend the hall at a cost of £1500. His work was obviously to his patron's liking, as he returned in 1851-2, further enlarging the house. It was illustrated in *The Builder* in 1881.

The second baronet, also Sir James, inherited in 1883 and largely rebuilt the house 1885-87, creating its final form with a large addition to the north. It was no architectural masterpiece but what it lacked in style, its fifty-four rooms made up for in size.

The third Sir James died in 1900, within a year of succeeding to his father's title but it was the activities of his son Sir

(1) Entrance Front (E. Todd)

(2) South Front 1955 (H. Ballard)

(3) From South East (W. Miers)

Robert which have become legendary.

He inherited at the age of ten and on joining the Coldstream Guards in the First World War was said to be the richest man in the British Army. Fond of both wine and women, he also developed a passion for railways and fire engines. In the 1920's he built the 7-mile Sand Hutton Light Railway with a branch line to the hall from Sand Hutton Central. Motive power was provided by two engines named after his wives. His private fire brigade put out few blazes but at one dinner party Sir Robert appeared in fireman's uniform, complete with brass helmet and proceeded to hose down Lady Walker at the table.

He died in 1930 and the estate, but not the house, was sold to the Church Commissioners. During the war it was requisitioned for use by Polish servicemen. It was subsequently sold by the family and in 1955 the new owners auctioned the southern half for the materials, including the turf on the lawn. The northern part of the building, including the tower, survived as flats but was demolished in 1971.

(4) Staircase 1955 (H. Ballard)

(5) North Front - detail 1964 (C. R. Evers)

11

CLAXTON HALL

The design suggests an early 18th century house, stuccoed and altered in the early 19th century. In 1851 it became a private lunatic asylum. In 1872 it was the seat of Frederick Walker, second son of Sir James Walker Bt., of Sand Hutton Hall (q.v.).

From 1924 it was an Army hiring but the War Office bought it in 1940. It became a military hospital in 1943. From 1947 to 1981 it was the official residence of G.O.C. Northern Command. On Christmas Eve of that year it burnt down, shortly after being sold by the Ministry of Defence.

South Front 1981 (Smiths Gore)

HILDENLEY HALL

William Strickland acquired the Hildenley estate in 1565. The house his descendants built in 1620 had later embellishments including refenestration and the heavy pedimented door surround. The west wing was dated 1768.

Hidden away below a wooded bank, it provided the perfect retreat for the reclusive orchid-growing Sir Charles Strickland Bt. By the time he died in 1909 it was in poor repair. It was bought by the Hon. Francis Dawnay and largely demolished 1927-31. Today it is a scene of eerie ruins, with palm trees still growing where they were planted in the orchid houses.

South Front (D. Barran)

EASTHORPE HALL

The Hebdens' house enjoyed spectacular views over the rolling acres of Castle Howard's parkland. There had been a house on the site for many years and the park was walled by Lord Eure in 1617-20. James Hebden had moved to the old house by 1755. He rebuilt (or at least remodelled) the house shortly afterwards.

For many years it was attributed to John Carr but more recent scholars have suggested Thomas Atkinson. Whoever was responsible impressed Pevsner sufficiently for him to call it "uncommonly fine". The house, as built, had a canted bay window on the south front with three arched windows, themselves flanked by Venetian windows. What made this front all the more extraordinary was the fact that all the windows had Gibb surrounds. The main entrance to the west had Tuscan columns, fluted frieze and pediment. Internally there was a good staircase.

On the death of James Hebden's grandson, also James, it was sold and absorbed into the Castle Howard estate. Various worthies occupied it as tenants in the 19th century and Charles Smithson entertained his friend Charles Dickens here in the summer of 1843.

In 1926 it was massively but successfully enlarged by the 3rd Lord Grimthorpe, to the designs of Walter Brierley. A seven bay north front housed the new entrance, surmounted by the Grimthorpe arms in a pediment. After the family sold the house in 1965, it became a night club and was burnt down in mysterious circumstances in 1971.

(1) North Front 1927 (Lord Grimthorpe)

(2) South Front 1927 (Lord Grimthorpe)

WIGANTHORPE HALL

The village of Wiganthorpe in the Howardian Hills disappeared early and by 1377 there were only twelve adults. In 1304 Sir Miles Stapleton, already the owner of most of the main manor, gained the hunting. The Stapletons were succeeded by the Methams who rebuilt the hall in the 17th century. After the Methams came the Geldarts, who bought the estate in the 1660's and owned the estate for most of the 18th century.

John Carr produced designs for a new house in about 1780. His client was William Garforth, the new owner of Wiganthorpe. The Garforths hailed from Garforth Hall (dem.) at Ryton near Malton and rose to prominence and great wealth in the 18th century.

Carr's proposal was for a large square block to the south of the existing hall. Five bays wide and seven deep, with a large two-storey bay on the south front, it presented an austere exterior, with steeply falling ground to the south and east emphasising its squareness. Unlike the old stone hall, which became the kitchen wing, the new house was in red brick with stone facings. There was little apparent attempt to blend one with the other, to the extent that Whellan, writing in 1859, described it as "... the old hall with a modern one attached to it". Later alterations to the west front softened the contrast between the two.

Internally, Wiganthorpe was John Carr at his best. The plasterwork was, in its restrained late 18th century way, outstanding and the quality of the fireplaces and other fittings could not be faulted. The staircase with its Ionic columns and cantilevered flights leading up to an arcaded landing, followed a

familiar Carr pattern.

William Garforth's nephew, Commander William R.N., bred bloodstock when he inherited the estate; his grandson William Henry was the last member of the family to own Wiganthorpe. In 1890 he sold the estate to the Hon. William Henry Wentworth who was engaged to Earl Fitzwilliam's daughter, Lady Mary. Extensive works were carried out and various external alterations probably date from this time.

William Wentworth-Fitzwilliam died in 1920 and the following year the estate was sold to Lord Holden of Alston. In 1937 the estate was sold and subsequently split.

In 1953 the house was bought by a speculator who sold it to a breaker for £6000. In 1955 Wiganthorpe doors were fetching £100 apiece and the staircase was removed to Sharow Hall near Ripon. The kitchen wing and stables remain.

(1) View from the South West c.1900 (R. Walker)

(2) The Adam Hall 1953

(3) The Staircase Hall 1953

(4) The Drawing Room 1953

DALBY HALL

Dalby Hall perched on a high escarpment on the edge of the Howardian Hills. Its origins are scantly recorded and its disappearance in 1961 was hardly noticed.

By the time its end came, the house had been much altered, but the disintegrating render of later years revealed massive stone quoins up to the first floor level. These, together with blocked window openings and its H-plan, suggest (in line with local tradition) a 17th century house. It is also said to have contained a drawing room with early panelling. Refenestration and drastic alterations to the upper floor and roof probably date from the late 18th or early 19th century.

The Lumley family were long associated with Dalby and it was still in the possession of their relations the Ewbanks in the mid 19th century.

By 1890 it formed part of W. H. Garforth's nearby Wiganthorpe estate (q.v.) and had declined to the status of a farmhouse, tenanted by a Mr. Ponsonby. Vacant through much of the 1950's, it had reached an advanced state of decay and in 1961 the new owners were advised by their architect that it would cost as much to restore the house as it would to demolish and build anew. In the spirit of the times, they chose the latter. The 18th century stables remain.

(1) View from the South 1954 (Mrs. Elvin)

(2) South Front 1961 (W. H. Helm)

16

RISEBOROUGH HALL

The house was gutted by fire in 1952 and the 17th century parlour wing still lies in ruins, although a new house has been created within the shell of the remainder.

The old wing has a rainwater head dated 1664 but some of the fittings were earlier in style, suggesting that the builder was Sir Arthur Robinson, a London merchant, who bought the property in 1632.

By the mid 19th century it was just a tenanted farmhouse. In 1878 the Robinsons sold the house to Thomas Harrison who replaced the older Hall wing and added bay windows to the garden front.

South Front (T. L. Frank)

SLINGSBY CASTLE

A castellated mansion of an Elizabethan type standing on the site of the Hastings' castle. The architect was John Smithson and Pevsner dates it to the 1620's. The central oblong block has four turrets at the corners and vaulted kitchens below. Surprisingly, for such a large house, its builder, Sir Charles Cavendish, was a dwarf. He died in 1653.

It passed into the hands of the Duke of Newcastle, then the Duke of Buckingham but was left uninhabited and fell into decay. In 1751 it was bought by the Earl of Carlisle and its ruins still form part of the Castle Howard estate.

Slingsby Castle 1990

KELDY CASTLE

Keldy Castle, like other moorside lodges, was a product of 19th century wealth, spent on the increasingly fashionable sport of shooting. It lay in an isolated position to the north of Pickering. Its lifeblood for 140 years was the prosperity of Hull, which provided the funds for its owners to indulge in a holiday home on the grand scale.

Keldy Castle lay at the centre of an estate with modest enough beginnings; Hull banker William Liddell bought a farmhouse known as Keldy Grange with 266 acres in 1810.

Liddell's aggrandisement of his purchase consisted of a three-bay castellated central block built, like the rest of the building, out of native freestone and faced with Portland cement. There were hooded mouldings over the windows and to the east, a corner turret, a two-storeyed bay window and further turrets beyond.

The architect is not known but the design bears a striking resemblance to Cave Castle, in the East Riding, designed by Henry Hakewill for Henry Barnard.

William Liddell began buying the surrounding land and on his death his heirs followed the same path, assiduously creating a sporting estate which by the closing years of the century extended to over 8000 acres.

The sale catalogue of 1893 describes the house as a 'bijou castellated residence' with three principal rooms and ten principal bedrooms. The successful bidder at the sale was Sir James Reckitt Bt., a Hull industrialist whose fortune came from Reckitt & Colman, the firm founded by his father Isaac.

In 1900 Sir James' second son Philip married Hilda Grotian, and was given the

18

Keldy estate as a wedding present. Philip added a rather institutional two-storey block to the west of the old house and in 1910 William Anelays, the York master builders started work on what was to become the main block. The architect was John Bilson of Hull.

Liddell's castle was all but obliterated and replaced with a large Tudor-style house, four bays wide and flanked by two shallow projecting wings. A large square tower rose up from behind. Bilson's interior, like so much of his work, was of the highest order. Gardens, including an elaborate water garden, were laid out to the south.

It was never used for more than a few weeks of the year. During the Second World War it was requisitioned by the Army and proved an unpopular posting due to its remoteness. Sir Philip Reckitt died in 1944 and in 1946 his executors sold it to the Forestry Commission for use as a Forestry School. Following a change of mind, it became surplus to requirements and was demolished, not without difficulty, in 1950.

Keldy Castle c.1904 (R. Allanson)

Keldy Castle c.1908 (R. Allanson)

Keldy Castle c.1912 (R. Allanson)

Keldy Castle 1950 (R. Allanson)

MEADOWFIELD, Whitby

Meadowfield was the home of the Simpsons, a family of successful Whitby businessmen. 'Simpson, Chapman and Co.' was one of several local banking houses which sprang up in the late 18th century, and it was the longest-lasting, being absorbed by the York Union Bank as late as 1892. Wakefield Simpson (d.1806), grocer and draper, went into partnership with Abel Chapman about 1785, and they established their bank in Grape Lane in old Whitby, overlooking the harbour. Wakefield Simpson was succeeded by his son, grandson and great-grandson (Henry Simpson, who was a director from 1848 to 1892). Henry Simpson died at Meadowfield in 1893. Later in the 20th century, the house was owned by the Marwood family of shipowners.

Little is known about Meadowfield's architectural history. Its late 18th century appearance suggests that Wakefield Simpson, having prospered in commerce, bought land at the edge of the town and built the house. It was of brick, with a prominent and somewhat elongated Venetian window above the entrance porch. In style it was somewhat similar to another house on the edge of Whitby, Low Stakesby Hall. The gable and parapet, which occurred on the garden front also, seem to have been of a different brick and may have been a later alteration.

The interiors were altered in a heavy Victorian style in the late 19th century, probably for Henry Simpson. One room had elaborate Chinese wallpaper of birds in trees, which may have survived from an earlier decorative scheme. The dark fireplace and overmantel, with vigorous

carving, was typical of such features installed in most rooms in the house. The rooms on the garden front had large bay windows framed with dark wood and with stained glass panels of musicians and other artists in the upper lights. The drawing room had a richly plastered ceiling and frieze.

Meadowfield was demolished in the mid-1950's and the site was completely built over.

(1) North front (RCHM England)

(2) Chinese room (RCHM England)

(3) Drawing room (RCHM England)

(4) Window detail (RCHM England)

KIRKLEATHAM HALL
Redcar

The seat of the Turners was demolished in 1954, a sad loss in a village full of their monuments. It was a mid-17th century house remodelled in Gothick style by John Carr of York in 1764-7.

John Turner (d.1643) purchased the Kirkleatham estate in 1623. His son John Turner (1613-88) built the Hall shown in Knyff and Kip's engraving. It was H-shaped with a cupola and elaborate Dutch gables. Samuel Buck's sketch, 1720, showed the weather vane bearing the date 1669, perhaps the date of the building (or perhaps commemorating Turner's brother Sir William, Lord Mayor of London in that year). Buck shows one addition to the wings of the house, whereas Knyff and Kip show two: the left-hand one may have been their invention. There were formal gardens beyond the stable range, and walled gardens; and beside them was the Hospital, founded by Sir William Turner in 1676.

James Gibbs made unexecuted designs for a classical house in the 1730's. In 1764 Charles Turner (1727-83) commissioned John Carr, who had recently altered Turner's Clints Hall, Swaledale [q.v.] to remodel Kirkleatham. Carr filled out the centre of the Hall and added wings, the east wing with a large bow window. The material was brick, rough-cast, and the style Gothick. It was certainly not Carr's most elegant or successful design.

No plans of the Hall are known. The most striking room was the two-storey dining room, above the main staircase on the north side. Its coved ceiling was decorated with plasterwork designed by Carr and executed, presumably, by his

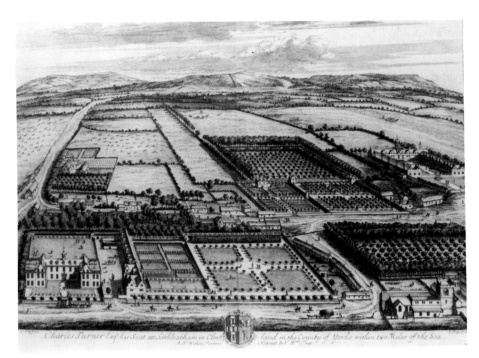

'Charles Turner Esq. his seat at Kirkleatham'. (Knyff and Kip, Britannia illustrata (1707).)

South front (Langbaurgh-on-Tees Museum Service, Kirkleatham Old Hall Museum, Redcar.)

22

usual plasterer, James Henderson. (Both Henderson and William Sutton & Co., plasterers, are mentioned in the accounts, and it is unclear who did what). The ceiling featured mythological scenes — perhaps a Bacchic procession — among festoons of foliage. The white and siena marble chimney pieces in the Hall were by Wilton. The gallery, which occupied the east wing, was plainer. The striking Corinthian doorcase, designed, according to Arthur Young, by Sir William Chambers, was perhaps inspired by a plate in Chambers' *Treatise on Civil Architecture* (1759). Near the gallery was a 'Chinese room' with Chinese wallpaper and lacquered furniture.

The grounds were landscaped in the 18th century. The stables, of the 1730's with additions by Carr, Carr's Gothick entrance archway, and the boundary bastions (recalling Castle Howard) remain, but an octagonal temple with rococo plasterwork, dating perhaps from the 1740's, was demolished in the 1950's. On the hill to the south were grottoes, cascades and temples, all obliterated, and near the Hall, an ambitious Gothick dovecote, of Carr's time, if not of his design.

The Hall was little changed thereafter. It passed from Sir Charles Turner (1773-1810) to his widow, who married Henry Vansittart, to their daughter Teresa Newcomen (1813-87), and finally to her granddaughter, Kathleen Le Roy Lewis. The Hall was occupied intermittently in the 20th century, and after Mrs. Le Roy Lewis's death in 1948 the contents were sold. The Hall passed through several hands, but no satisfactory use could be found for it. It fell into disrepair and was sold for its fittings and materials in 1954.

Dining room (RCHM England.)

Gallery (RCHM England.)

OLD HALL
Guisborough

Knyff and Kip's view shows the 18th century home of the Chaloners. William Chaloner (1655-1715) moved from Park House to the Hall in the grounds of the former Priory. The triple gable ends and former windows indicate an older house, to which Chaloner added an unsymmetrical front with sash windows. The formal gardens, with parterres and avenues, a pyramidal duck-decoy and a fountain west of the Hall, were landscaped later in the 18th century.

Financial difficulties obliged Robert Chaloner to sell the Hall for its materials c.1805. The Chaloners moved to a farmhouse, Long Hull, on the site of the present Hall.

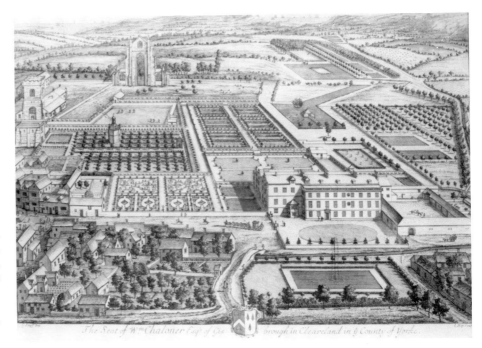

'The Seat of Wm. Chaloner Esq.,' from the west. (Knyff and Kip, Britannia illustrata (1707).)

TOCKETTS HALL
Guisborough

Tocketts Hall (Plantation House) was the home of General John Hale (1728-1806), who fought with Wolfe at Quebec. The Tocketts family lived there from Norman times; the old hall had a private chapel. George Tocketts sold the estate in 1815. It passed to the Chaloners of Guisborough. General Hale married Mary Chaloner in 1763. Plantation Farm was her dowry; Hale bought Tocketts Hall. He made many additions (to house 21 children?). The most interesting feature was a squat tower with lunette windows. A ground plan, known in 1905, is now lost. Tocketts, repurchased by Robert Chaloner (1809), was demolished c.1815.

Tocketts Hall (Guisborough Museum)

24

PARK HOUSE
Guisborough

The Chaloners, who have owned the Guisborough estate since 1550, lived first at Park House, high on the hills north-west of the town. There was a medieval deer park, which was stocked with deer until the 18th century. In the 1662 Hearth Tax assessment Park House was returned as having 14 hearths; in the 1673 assessment it had 17. Sir Edward Chaloner (d.1680) was then the owner, and his son William Chaloner (1655-1715) was the occupant. It was William Chaloner who removed his residence to the Old Hall. Thereafter Park House was held mostly by tenants; the dining room was retained for the use of shooting parties. It was abandoned, became derelict, and was demolished c.1970.

Park House was substantial and old, a rectangular stone building with central projections north and south. On the north side were two huge flues, with seven (not 17) chimneys. The ground floor of the 'tower' on this side had a good classical window. The original windows had flat hood-moulds. The 18th-century hipped roof cut off the tops of the topmost ovals, and the hood-moulds of the top-storey windows had been lost. This, together with the Hearth Tax assessments, suggest that Park House was once higher — perhaps by another storey — and had a more varied roofline.

(1) South front (S.K. Chapman)

(2) North front (J. Brelstaff)

UPLEATHAM HALL,
Guisborough

Upleatham was a rather unattractive house, well sited on rising ground in a valley north-east of Guisborough. The main phases of its architectural history are known, but the details are somewhat conjectural. So far as is known, no ground plans or photographs survive to indicate the internal arrangement of the Hall. It was demolished in 1897.

Upleatham was a Cleveland seat of the Dundas family, Earls and later Marquesses of Zetland. Their Cleveland estates included also Marske and Loftus, the halls of which survive. The family was Scottish. Sir Lawrence Dundas, (d.1782) son of Thomas Dundas of Edinburgh and Stirling, made a fortune in government service, (especially as an army contractor during the Seven Years War, 1757-63), purchased the Cleveland estates in 1762-4, and the Aske and Richmond estates from Lord Holdernesse of Hornby Castle [q.v.] in 1762.

Sir Lawrence's son, Sir Thomas Dundas (1741-1820), 1st Lord Dundas (1794) occupied Upleatham Hall during his father's lifetime. The appearance of the old Hall is not known. Samuel Buck did not sketch it. Sir Thomas commissioned John Carr (who had altered Aske Hall for Sir Lawrence Dundas) to enlarge the house. The date is unclear. Sir Thomas married Lady Charlotte Fitzwilliam in 1764, so perhaps the work was done soon after that. It is probable that the section of the house with two pediments represents Carr's work. If so, it is clearly unbalanced, suggesting either that Carr intended to complete the remodelling later, or that part of it was subsequently demolished.

Upleatham Hall from the north-west (Langbaurgh-on-Tees Museum Service)

North front (Langbaurgh-on-Tees Museum Service)

Lord Dundas's heir, Lawrence Dundas (1766-1839), 1st Earl of Zetland (1838), married Harriet Hale, a daughter of General John Hale of neighbouring Plantation House or Tocketts Hall [q.v.]. He lived at Marske, and in 1810 it was presumably he who commissioned Sir Robert Smirke to enlarge Upleatham Hall. The large west block, cubical and plainly detailed, was probably Smirke's design. When Thomas Dundas (1795-1873) succeeded as 2nd Earl of Zetland in 1839, it seems that he made various additions to the south side of the Hall. A weakly Italianate bell appeared over a curious first floor arcade. This may have given access to a roof garden over a single-storey room, which led from Smirke's block to a large conservatory. Smirke's block acquired a bay window. It is tempting to ascribe all these features to Ignatius Bonomi of Durham, but all that is known for certain is that he laid an oak parquet floor in the dining room about 1840. The pool, fountain and Italian garden may have been later still, added perhaps in the time of Lawrence Dundas, 3rd Earl of Zetland (1st Marquess, 1892).

The Duke of Sussex, son of George III, was a frequent visitor to Upleatham. The last visitors were Lord and Lady Fitzwilliam, who spent part of their honeymoon there in 1895. Soon afterwards the walls of the Hall began to give way. The ironstone boom had led to a mine being opened in the hillside close to the Hall. The subsidence destroyed not only the Hall but much of the village of Upleatham also. The Hall was dismantled and demolished in 1897. The stone ha-ha of the park is almost the only surviving trace.

View from the north-east (Cleveland Archives)

South front (Langbaurgh-on-Tees Museum Service)

LINTHORPE, BLUE HALL
Middlesbrough

'Linthrope the Seat of Peter Consett Gent.', sketched by Samuel Buck in c.1720, survived long enough to be photographed. It was demolished in 1870, when Middlesbrough was beginning to expand into neighbouring hamlets. By 1870 it seems to have become a farmhouse. It had changed little since Buck sketched it: an L-shaped house of brick, with stone dressings. It may have been part of an intended larger house, begun but never completed. The crossed mullions and transoms of many of the windows indicate a late 17th century building. By 1870 some of the windows had been replaced with 18th century sashes. Peter Consett is not mentioned in genealogies of the Consetts. In Buck's time, William Consett is described as 'of Linthorpe'. Perhaps Peter was his father, or a brother. Two of William Consett's sons married daughters of William Pennyman of Normanby, near Middlesbrough, and obtained estates there. The subsequent descent of the Blue Hall, Linthorpe, is not definitely known.

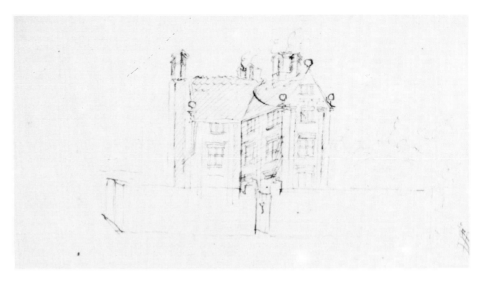

(1) Samuel Buck, 'Linthrope The Seat of Peter Consett Gent.' (British Library, Lansdowne mss. 914.)

(2) Linthorpe from the south-east (Cleveland Archives.)

28

STAINSBY HALL
Middlesbrough

Stainsby Hall, north of Stainton in Cleveland, disappeared so long ago that Samuel Buck's sketch of c.1720 seems to be the only record. It was for several centuries the seat of the Gower family, and later passed into the hands of the Turners of Kirkleatham. In 1720 it was the seat of John Turner, and later was owned by the Lascelles family.

It was a substantial 17th century house of some architectural distinction. A three-bay centre had a central projecting porch. Two wings projected, and two corner pavilions, with open arcades on the ground floor, projected still further forward.

Samuel Buck, 'The East Prospect of Stainsby the Seat of John Turner esq.' (British Library, Lansdowne mss. 914.)

THORNTON HALL,
Stainton-in-Cleveland

Thornton Hall was demolished presumably because, as the subsidiary house of the Pennyman family of Ormesby Hall, no use could be found for it. Samuel Buck's sketch of c.1720 seems to be the only record of it. It was then the seat of Sir James Pennyman. It had vanished by the end of the 18th century. It was a substantial H-shaped house with gables and projecting wings. The use of decorative pilasters on the wings recalls the incomplete Linthorpe Hall [q.v.].

Samuel Buck, 'Thornton The Seat of Sir Jam. Pennyman Bart.' (British Library, Landsdowne mss.914.)

MARTON HALL
Middlesbrough

Henry Bolckow and John Vaughan transformed Middlesbrough from a struggling coal port into a metropolis of the iron industry. They quickly became wealthy, and, like most successful Victorian businessmen, sought suburban estates. In 1853 Bolckow bought the Marton Hall estate, a mile south of Middlesbrough.

Bolckow (1806-78) was a German from Sulten in East Prussia. After entering business at Rostock, he emigrated to Newcastle in 1827. There he formed a partnership with Vaughan, and they moved to Middlesbrough in 1839. Their small-scale ironworks were transformed by the discovery of ironstone in the Cleveland Hills in 1850.

The old house at Marton burnt down in 1832. Bartholomew Rudd of Marske bought the estate in 1786, and rebuilt Marton Lodge soon after. Its appearance does not seem to have been recorded. After the fire it was left as a shell, and the Rudds moved to Tollesby Hall. They sold Marton to the Revd. James A. Park in 1846, and he sold it to Bolckow in 1853.

The new Marton Hall was at first a rather plain classical red-brick house, a main block with portico and balustraded parapet, and subsidiary ranges to one side. The transition was marked by a gaunt octagonal tower capped by a dome. On the garden front was a cast-iron verandah and balcony, a colonnade, and a conservatory.

Bolckow was Middlesbrough's first Mayor (1853) and its first M.P. (1867). He presented the Albert Park to the town, and in 1868 Prince Arthur came to open it. In preparation for the royal visit, Bolckow 'hotted up' his house in a heavy

Original north front, c.1860 (Cleveland County Library, Middlesbrough)

North front after 1867 (RCHM England)

French style. It is probable that the German architect Ludwig Martens, whom Bolckow was employing elsewhere on his estates in the 1860's, designed the alterations. Much decoration was applied: window-surrounds, string-courses, and statues above the portico and round the dome. Above the parapets, mansard roofs capped with intricate ironwork appeared, and the pediments of the main block's dormer-windows were supported by caryatids. A new glazed colonnade led to a hexagonal conservatory.

Bolckow decorated and furnished Marton lavishly. The hall had a black and white marble floor and columns of Carrara Marble. The staircase and balcony were also of Carrara. He made large purchases of sculpture, books, furniture, and pictures, including works by Landseer, Turner, Millais, Rosa Bonheur, and other 19th century artists. He bought many Captain Cook manuscripts, including the journal of the *Endeavour* expedition. Cook was born in a cottage at Marton demolished in 1786; in 1858 Bolckow marked the spot in his grounds with a huge granite vase.

Bolckow was succeeded in 1878 by his nephew Carl. In 1888 industrial recession forced Carl to sell his pictures and manuscripts. Marton was unoccupied for many years. Much of the furniture, and the books, were sold in 1907. Troops were stationed in the Hall in the 1914-18 War. The remaining contents were sold in 1924, and the estate was bought in 1925 by Thomas J. Stewart, who presented it to Middlesbrough as a park. The Hall was for a time a museum, then the fire-service headquarters. It deteriorated, and in 1960 began to be demolished. In the course of demolition it was gutted by fire.

Original south front, c.1860 (Cleveland County Library, Middlesbrough)

South front after 1867 (Cleveland County Council, Dept. of Economic Development & Planning.)

GUNNERGATE HALL
Marton, Middlesbrough

Original house, c.1860 (Cleveland County Library, Middlesbrough)

Bolckow and Vaughan, ironmasters, bought neighbouring estates near Middlesbrough. Gunnergate, John Vaughan's seat, was a brick house, Gothic with many gables, built in 1857 for the Quaker banker Charles Leatham (d.1858). His widow sold it to Vaughan in 1860. When Vaughan died in 1868, his son Thomas doubled the size of the house and fitted it up extravagantly. The *Evening Gazette* noted (30 August 1870) 'a complete revolution.. Magnificent dining, drawing and billiard rooms.. pillars of polished Aberdeen granite.. the gardens, greenhouses, vineries, etc., have been greatly extended.. Gunnergate Hall will take its place among the stately homes of Cleveland.' The architect (who might also have designed Leatham's house) is unknown. The main rooms were fronted by a Gothic arcade. It was said that the billiard room cost £40,000, and a bedstead £1500. Vaughan's company crashed in 1879. Work on a banquetting hall and ballroom ceased and house and contents were sold. There are no interior photographs but the *Northern Echo* (2 June 1879), described at length 'the reign of the son when money was spent as freely as the outpouring of water... Sumptuous furniture, costly hangings, and carpets, inlaid doors, stencilled walls, and gilded ceilings.' The Hall was bought by Carl Bolckow, nephew of Henry Bolckow, in 1881. In 1888 he too was forced to retrench and sold Gunnergate to Sir Raylton Dixon, shipbuilder. Dixon died in 1901 and his widow left the house. Gunnergate was never lived in again. It was occupied by the Army in both wars, and was demolished in 1946.

Gunnergate after 1870 (Cleveland County Council, Dept. of Economic Development & Planning.)

TOLLESBY HALL
Marton, Middlesbrough

There was a 16th or 17th century Hall at Tollesby; but no views of it are known. Lord Lonsdale sold the estate to Bartholomew Rudd of Marton Hall in 1803, and Rudd built the new Tollesby Hall on a site some distance from the old Hall. It was called 'newly erected' in 1808. It was of five bays with pediment and balustraded parapets, and lower, two-bay wings. The recessed entrance porch may have been a later alteration. Major John B. Rudd owned Tollesby for many years, but sold it in 1886. He made numerous alterations which created a rather rambling effect. He was an amateur architect and stonemason, and used these skills in his restoration of Marton Church. At his 1886 sale a newspaper observed that 'although Major Rudd has been altering and repairing his residence during the whole of his tenure of the estate, he has not yet completed the work.' Whellan (1859) records that Tollesby had been 'recently enlarged'. In 1886 Rudd left plans for further 'improvements', including a tower. There was already an octagonal tower adjoining an enlarged wing. Perhaps Rudd hoped to replace the surviving original wing and its smaller, square tower. On the garden front Rudd added a canted projection with off-centre doorway and an awkward, arched window above. In 1886 Tollesby was bought by James Emerson of Easby Hall. It passed to his son, Eleazer Biggins Emerson, but later became a builder's yard. It was demolished in 1984 to make way for a housing estate for expanding Middlesbrough.

North front (R. Cook)

South front (J. H. Cousans)

ROUNTON GRANGE
East Rounton

The most original North Riding house of the late 19th century was built for Sir Lowthian Bell (d.1904), scientist and ironmaster. Bell bought the East Rounton estate from John Wailes in 1866, and at first wished to enlarge the brick farm-house on the site. By 1871 he had decided to rebuild. He had already employed the architect Philip Webb (1831-1915) for additions to Washington Hall, and Webb designed the vernacular-style Red Barns, Redcar, for Bell's son Hugh in 1868. The old Grange was closely flanked by mature trees which Sir Lowthian Bell wished to preserve. Webb was obliged to design within this constraint, and the result was a tall and striking tower-house. It was somewhat inspired by North Country and Scottish pele-towers, but there was more than a hint of Vanburgh (whom Webb admired) in the busy and massive skyline of gables and chimneystacks, and possibly a little continental feeling in the corner-pavilions with their pyramidal roofs. Gothic and classical detailing, white-framed sash windows and vernacular pantiles, co-existed happily. The stone was a warm honey-coloured sandstone from a nearby quarry. A clock-tower fronting the service wing was crowned by a jaunty spired turret.

The main rooms were panelled in light oak. Webb's colleagues William Morris and Sir Edward Burne-Jones designed the decorative scheme of the dining room. The ceiling was richly painted with an intricate floral pattern, and above the panelling was a tapestry frieze illustrating the Romaunt of the Rose, painstakingly embroidered by Lady Bell and her daughter Florence Johnson between 1872

South front (R. Cook)

East front (R. Cook)

34

and 1880. Above the sideboard, the pilgrim dreamed amongst roses in the garden of idleness: on one side he saw himself led by Danger, on the other by Love. On the fireplace wall, figures represented the Miseries of Life: Hate, Villainy, Avarice, Hypocrisy, and so forth. Opposite were figures representing the Joys of Life: Mirth, Gladness, Beauty, Love, Courtesy, etc. Elsewhere in the house was a notable 19th century picture collection, including *The Romans leaving Britain* by Millais, portraits by Watts and Richmond, landscapes by Hunt, and watercolours by Boyce, Hunt and De Wint.

Bell later employed George Jack, Philip Webb's long-serving assistant, to enlarge Rounton. From the dining room a long gallery led behind the clock tower to a large, barrel-vaulted common room, panelled in light oak like the rest of the house. This large and airy room must have provided a striking contrast with the dark, richly-decorated dining room. George Jack himself carved the wooden panels around the fireplace, the side panels illustrating the Supports of Life (phases of iron-making), and the top panels the Pleasures of Life.

Sir Lowthian Bell died in 1904, and his son, Sir Hugh, did not long outlive him. The payment of two sets of death duties, as well as economic and industrial difficulties, made Rounton too expensive to maintain. From the 1920's the family lived mostly at Mount Grace Manor. In the 1939-45 War the house was an evacuee home and later a hostel for Italian prisoners. Attempts to sell Rounton after the War were unsuccessful, and the National Trust would not accept it without an endowment. It was dismantled and demolished in 1954.

Dining room (Country Life)

Common room (Country Life)

CLERVAUX CASTLE,
Croft

Clervaux was a castellated mansion built for Sir William Chaytor, Bart., in 1839-44. It was designed by Ignatius Bonomi of Durham, who had already done work for Chaytor in the fashionable spa-town of Croft. In the early part of the commission Bonomi was assisted by his pupil, John Loughborough Pearson, who was a favourite of Chaytor's and hoped to become Bonomi's partner. Early in 1842 Bonomi went into partnership with John Cory, and Pearson left suddenly.

Clervaux's stiff and somewhat grim exterior suggested a late Gothic fortress — the partly ruined Snape Castle near Bedale was a possible model — with a keep-like porte-cochère, and square turrets arranged along its L-shaped range. Bonomi himself described the design (in a letter to Chaytor) as 'sober and majestic looking, not frittered into small parts, a fault frequently met with in modern castles'.

The reception rooms, which lay in the south range, were inspired by illustrations in Joseph Nash's *Mansions of England in olden times*, and incorporated, amidst modern oak panelling, genuinely antique mantelpieces and a staircase from the old Mansion House in Newcastle. The plaster ceilings, geometric patterns decorated with fruit and foliage, were executed by R. Taylor of Richmond. The stables and coach-house, with a tall clock tower, were built in 1844-7, and are the only part of the Castle to survive.

After Sir William Chaytor's death in 1847, Clervaux was occupied by his daughters, one of whom, Harriet Chaytor, survived into the 1890's. The Castle was left to Sir William Chaytor of the Old

Hall, Croft, (d. 1896). In the early 20th century it was occupied by George May, a hunting man; and in the 1920's, by Alfred Chaytor, a grandson of the builder. After his death in about 1935 it stood empty until requisitioned by the army in the 1939-45 War. Afterwards there were suggestions that the newly-formed Coal Board might buy it, or that it might be turned into flats for the homeless. While it was empty, however, the lead was stolen from the roofs, and the owner, C. W. D. Chaytor, sold it to Baharie Brothers of Sunderland. They demolished it in 1950, the stonework being broken up for road-building material.

(1) South-west view (W. D. Chaytor)

(2) Library (Mrs. Reid)

(3) Dining room (W. D. Chaytor)

GATHERLEY CASTLE
Middleton Tyas

Designer and date of Gatherley are uncertain. Sash-windows and hoodmoulds suggest c.1830-40; but Whellan (1859) does not mention it. Was John Middleton of Darlington the architect? Or did Sir Henry de Burgh-Lawson (1817-92), self-styled baronet, owner in the 1870's and a naval architect, design it himself? Mr. Coatsworth of Darlington occupied Gatherley after 1892; Mary Barmingham (1860-1915), daughter of Darlington ironmaster William Barmingham, bought it in 1900. After her death it was unoccupied. The furniture was sold in 1928. Gatherley was requisitioned in 1939-45. Later no use could be found, and it was demolished in 1963.

Gatherley Castle (The Northern Echo)

HALNABY HALL
Croft

Halnaby Hall, south of Darlington, was perhaps most famous as the scene of Lord Byron's disastrous honeymoon in January 1815. He had married Annabella, daughter of Sir Ralph Milbanke, but regretted it immediately, since he was in love with his half-sister Augusta Leigh. The miserable month which the ill-suited pair spent at Halnaby has been recounted many times, particularly by Ethel Colburn Mayne in her *Life of Lady Byron*.

Mark Milbanke (d.1677), a Durham alderman, bought the Halnaby estate from Sir Francis Boynton in 1649. Boynton had acquired it through the female line from the Place family in 1633; and Robert Place had received it on his marriage to the last of the Halnaby family, Katherine, in 1410. Parts of the old house, in late Gothic style, survived in the service wing of Halnaby. The main house was rebuilt by Mark Milbanke, or by his son Sir Mark Milbanke, Bart. (d.1680) after 1660. It was a tall, square, three-storey block, of brick with stone dressings. The original fenestration— mullioned and transomed windows, capped by pediments — could be seen in the uppermost windows. The lower ones were converted to sashes, re-using the pediments, in 1728 or earlier. The main entrance to the house was on the north side, through a columned porch of two storeys with pierced balustrades. The porch had the correct hierarchy of Orders in its capitals — Doric on the ground

(1) Halnaby from the north-east (Country Life)

(2) South-east view (The Northern Echo)

38

floor, Ionic above, and Corinthian in the applied decoration flanking the top window.

Celia Fiennes described Halnaby in 1698 as 'a house of Sir Mark Melborn on a hill, a brick building several towers on the top...'; and a faint sketch in John Warburton's journal, 1719, shows Halnaby crowned with a small cupola. He also shows the east wing already built in 1718, and a low building in front of it forming an entrance courtyard. The west wing was not yet built: a jumble of old buildings is indicated. Halnaby was not sketched by Samuel Buck.

In c.1729 Sir Ralph Milbanke restored the symmetry of the house by rebuilding the west wing. It had rainwater-heads of this date. Sir Ralph had married Anne Delaval of Seaton Delaval in 1725, and since Sir John Vanbrugh was designing Seaton Delaval at that time, there have been unconvincing suggestions that he was involved at Halnaby. But the east wing, with its bay window and massive flanking chimneystacks, was already standing in 1725, and, although a striking and forceful design, it was conventional and showed no real Vanbrughian characteristics. The chimneystacks were decorated with pedimented niches and blank (but glazed) windows, and circular motifs in square panels above the parapet. A drawing room occupied the ground floor of this wing. The west wing, containing offices, merely fronted the old offices.

The columned porch opened into a corner of Halnaby's most splendid room, the hall. Later, when the entrance was

(3) Dining room (Country Life)

(4) Dining room during demolition (RCHM England)

moved to the south side, the hall became the dining room. This room, with its delicate rococo plasterwork, with panels containing female masks and festoons of fruit and flowers on the walls, and a swirling ceiling, dated probably from after 1748, when Sir Ralph Milbanke (son of the above) succeeded. The ceiling plasterwork was similar to a ceiling at Arncliffe Hall, Ingleby Arncliffe. The library, on the south side of the Hall, had more restrained plasterwork of the 1770's, and the staircase hall in the centre of the south front was remodelled for John Todd in the 1840's. The remodelling was skilfully done in a style compatible with that of 1730.

Halnaby was, fortunately, photographed by *Country Life* in 1933, when it was still furnished, and many of the rooms, with a wide variety of chimneypieces and furnishings, were illustrated. On the death of Sir Ralph Noel (he changed his name from Milbanke), Lady Byron's father, Halnaby passed to his nephew, Sir John Milbanke, who sold it in 1842 to John Todd of Tranby Park, with its furnishings. After the death of Lady Wilson Todd in the 1940's, Halnaby was bought by G. N. Gregory. It was offered for sale in 1951, but was unsold. In the following year the fixtures and fittings were sold, and the house was demolished. Much of the plasterwork of the dining room was transferred to the Bridge Inn, Walshford, where it was truncated and adapted to fit a smaller room. Part of the porch was rebuilt at Newsham House, and plasterwork from the drawing room ceiling is at Wycliffe Hall.

(5) Library (Country Life)

(6) Stair hall (Country Life)

GILMONBY HALL
Bowes, Barnard Castle

Situated high in Teesdale, Gilmonby was the seat of the Headlams from c.1750, to 1904. This old Teesdale family became shipbuilders in the 17th and 18th century, first at Stockton-on-Tees and later at Gateshead. Thomas Emerson Headlam quit shipbuilding and returned to Gilmonby Hall on his marriage in 1769. It was probably he who rebuilt (or at least refronted) the Hall, a rather plain building of three storeys and seven bays. The pedimented doorcase and the end bays with rusticated quoins were the only enrichments. The windows would originally have had glazing bars. Thomas Headlam's son John became Vicar of Wycliffe in 1793 and Archdeacon of Richmond in 1826. During his lifetime Gilmonby seems to have been let. Whellan (1858) records that it was first a boarding school and later a farmhouse. Thomas Emerson Headlam, the Archdeacon's son, resided occasionally at Gilmonby and probably embellished the grounds with terraces and a lake. In 1904 Gilmonby was sold to the Dugdale family. It was requisitioned in the 1939-45 War, and was demolished soon afterwards

(1) Gilmonby Hall, entrance front
(Mrs. L. Headlam-Morley)

(2) The terraces and lake
(Mrs. L. Headlam-Morley)

SEDBURY PARK
Gilling, Richmond

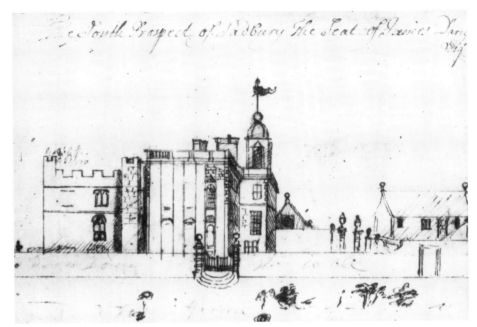

Sedbury, Pevsner wrote in *The Buildings of England*, 'looks early Victorian, but may be older'. He was misled, because the present house was built in 1928, replacing the old seat of the Darcys, the Hildyards and the Gilpin Browns. This fascinating house, part late medieval, part early 18th century, with alterations by Carr c.1770 and John Foss c.1799, was demolished in 1927.

In the 17th century James Darcy, youngest son of Conyers, Lord Darcy of Hornby Castle, acquired Sedbury on his marriage to Isabel Wyvill. Their son James, Lord Darcy of Navan (d.1733) left Sedbury to his cousin, whose daughter married Sir Robert Hildyard of Winestead, East Riding. Their son, Sir Robert Darcy Hildyard, preferred to live at Sedbury. On his death in 1814 Sedbury passed to James Darcy Hutton, who sold it in 1826 to John Gilpin, Vicar of Stockton. Gilpin's grandson George T. Gilpin Brown was the last occupant of Sedbury. He died in 1914 after stumbling in a rabbit hole when returning across fields from Scotch Corner.

Samuel Buck's sketch (1720) shows Sedbury much as it survived until the 1920's. There was an old range with Gothic windows and turrets and battlements. At right-angles was an early 18th century range, brick with stone dressings, balustraded parapets and a tall, square, domed lantern. Warburton, Buck's employer, visited James Darcy in 1718, noting that Sedbury was 'most of his own erecting'. The work slightly resembled Sir Abstrupus Danby's Swinton Park, begun in 1795, where (it is thought) Danby was his own architect. Sedbury's end-elevation

42

was a curious baroque design, three strips of rusticated stone set with round-headed windows, with triangular or segmental pediments hovering awkwardly over them. This elevation was emphatically two storeys high, but the side elevations, inexplicably, were of three storeys.

Two interior photographs are known. One shows the early 18th century staircase, the walls decorated with fluted composite pilasters, and with a plaster-work cornice and ceiling. The other shows John Carr's chaste dining room of c.1770, with attached Ionic columns. Sir Robert Hildyard, writing to John Grimston, described Carr's work for his son Robert Darcy Hildyard: 'Carr has indeed shown great skill in the Alterations of the old House at Sedbury, the Dining Room is 34F by 19 taken off by Columns, the Drawing Room above has a handsome Ceiling and Cornice and is elegantly furnished...' In the 1790's John Foss of Richmond made alterations, heightening the medieval turreted wing and altering its windows. In front of this wing a one-storey Gothic addition was made in the 19th century.

G. E. Sisterson bought Sedbury in 1919, and spent lavishly on 'improvements'. One of these, revealed by 1925 photographs, was to extend the house by one bay, moving the end elevation outwards and altering the strange baroque windows. His finances collapsed in 1925 and Sedbury was offered for sale at £12,000. In 1927 it was still unsold at the much reduced price of £4000. The house was auctioned for its fittings, and the shell was sold for £1100. A picture in the *Northern Echo*, 13 May 1927, showed Sedbury being demolished.

(1) Samuel Buck, 'The South Prospect of Sedbury The Seat of James Darcy esq' (British Library, Lansdowne mss.914)

(2) South-east view (H.C. Baker-Baker)

(3) Staircase and landing (Constable & Maude advertisement, Country Life, 14th March 1925)

(4) Dining room (Constable & Maude advertisement, Country Life, 14th March 1925)

STANWICK PARK
Aldbrough St. John

Stanwick was a 17th century house remodelled in Palladian style about 1740. A rainwater-head on the south front bore the date 1662. The house sketched by Samuel Buck in 1720 looked earlier than 1662, but perhaps the windows with crossed mullion and transom in the centre of the south front were altered then. The house was broadly H-shaped, with square domed corner turrets.

The Smithson family owned Stanwick from 1638. Sir Hugh Smithson (1714-1786) married Elizabeth, daughter of the 7th Duke of Somerset and great granddaughter of the last Percy Earl of Northumberland. Smithson acquired the vast Percy domains, and the revived earldom in 1750: he changed his name to Percy, and was created Duke of Northumberland in 1766.

A rainwater-head on the west side was dated 1740, the approximate date of the rebuilding of Stanwick. The 1740 architect is not definitely known. The 18th century estate account books, recorded in the library safe at Stanwick in 1870, but which cannot now be found, might have revealed details. Stanwick was clearly a building by one of Lord Burlington's circle, if not by Burlington himself. Daniel Garrett, Burlington's clerk of works, was invited to the North in 1737 by Smithson, Sir Thomas Robinson and the Earl of Carlisle. He remodelled Forcett Park Stanwick's neighbouring seat, and may have had a hand in Stanwick, but the

(1) Samuel Buck, 'Stanwicks Hall The Seat of Sr Hugh Smithson Bart.' (British Library, Lansdowne mss.914)

(2) South front after 1842 (The Duke of Northumberland)

44

design seems too good to be his. Sir Thomas Robinson, amateur architect, rebuilt his own seat at nearby Rokeby Park about 1730, and there are stylistic similarities between Rokeby and Stanwick. The strongest suggestion is, however, that William Kent (1685-1748), Burlington's close associate, was the designer. The west front parapet had triple open pediments, a device used by Kent elsewhere; yet the windows of this front broke through the first-floor string course in an un-Kentian way. (This may have been a later alteration, since photographs of the south front show that the windows there were not altered to break the string-course until c.1900).

The 1740 remodelling crowned the south front with a parapet. The main reception rooms were on the first floor. The saloon in the centre of the south front rose through two storeys. To the left was a small drawing room. In the centre of the west front, beneath the triple pediments, was the dining room. The ground floor windows on the south side had rusticated surrounds; about 1900 the central door was moved outwards to form a porch.

The attribution to William Kent is strengthened by the decoration of the dining room. The ceiling had heavy console brackets, an unusual feature used by Kent in the Blue Velvet Room at Chiswick, Lord Burlington's house. There was fine plasterwork also in the saloon. The walls had busts in niches, masks among swags and garlands, and palmy-panels going rococo. No photograph is known of the staircase, which Lady

(3) Saloon (The Duke of Northumberland)

(4) Dining room (Sale Catalogue; The Duke of Northumberland)

Oxford described in 1745 as 'fitted up with painting, stucco and gilding in a very pretty taste.'

A watercolour in a book of views of Percy properties gives a rather misleading impression of the house, but reveals a substantial summer house north of the pond, with a large arched opening beneath a plain pediment, and lower wings with arched openings.

In the 19th century Stanwick was the home of Lord Prudhoe, second son of the 2nd Duke, who succeeded as 4th Duke of Northumberland in 1847 and died in 1865. He commissioned Decimus Burton to add a low east wing and to remodel the servants' quarters and stables. Burton's more grandiose scheme for a carriage court, porticoed entrance and long processional corridor was not adopted.

After the 4th Duke's death his widow, 'Eleanor Duchess' lived at Stanwick, until her death in 1911. She laid out an Italian garden south of the house and a walled garden to the east. When she died, the historic furniture at Stanwick was sent to Alnwick Castle, and the house was occupied intermittently by Earl Percy and by tenants, the last being Colonel Wilson. In 1921 the estate was broken up to pay death duties. Colonel Wilson was not interested in buying the house. It was withdrawn at auction, and later sold to T. Place of Northallerton for £25,500. Two years later the fittings were sold (one room is now in the Minneapolis Institute of Arts) and Stanwick was demolished. The stable block and some of the service buildings survive.

(5) South-west view of Stanwick, from an 18th century watercolour (The Duke of Northumberland)

(6) West front, 19th century survey drawing (The Duke of Northumberland)

CARLTON HALL
Aldbrough St. John

Carlton Hall near Stanwick Park was purchased and rebuilt about 1800 by Samuel B. Moulton Barrett. The architect is unknown. Barrett sold Carlton to the Duke of Northumberland in 1828; it was the home of his agent in Richmondshire until Duchess Eleanor's death in 1911. The austere ashlar main block, with projecting porch, ground floor lunette windows and plain strip-pilasters, adjoined a lower and perhaps older rubblestone wing rather awkwardly. No interior views are known. Carlton housed German prisoners in the 1914-18 War and was demolished in 1919, four years before Stanwick Park.

Carlton Hall (per J. K. Gill)

CARLTON, ALDBRO'

GILLING WOOD HALL
Gilling, Richmond

In 1720 Buck sketched an early 17th century house with gables and front and side projections. The present Gillingwood Hall farmhouse has a Doric pedimented doorway from the old Hall, and nearby is a classical pavilion (the Tea House). These remains suggest a rebuilding of the Hall c.1730-40. It was burnt down in 1750. One story suggests that Margaret Wharton, who lived there, dismayed that her brother William did not bequeath it to her, threw a party, got drunk, and started the blaze. Alternatively, Cape the housekeeper stole the Whartons' valuables, and started the fire to conceal her crime.

Samuel Buck, 'Gillingwood The Seat of Will. Wharton Esqr.' (British Library, Lansdowne mss. 914)

HORNBY CASTLE Bedale

One range of Hornby Castle still stands, but its interiors were reconstructed in the 1930's. The other ranges of this great courtyard house, seat of the Lords Conyers, the Earls of Holdernesse and the Dukes of Leeds, were demolished in 1930.

According to Leland, Hornby was 'but a meane thing' before William, 1st Lord Conyers, rebuilt it about 1500. Samuel Buck's sketch (1720) shows the basic shape of Conyers' house, with a keep-like tower at the north-west corner, and the St. Quintin Tower at the south-east. In the south range was the arched courtyard entrance and an oriel window.

The main entrance was a splendid survival from Lord Conyers' rebuilding. On the north side of the courtyard, it bore his arms and coronet, vigorously carved, above the arched doorway. In 1930 the doorway was bought by the American tycoon William Randolph Hearst, but Sir William Burrell acquired it in 1953, and it is now in the Burrell Collection in Glasgow. Flanking the doorway were two other Gothic features, a part-octagonal projection with traceried windows, and a screen made up in the 18th century to hide an underground servants' passage which crossed the courtyard.

Buck showed a wing projecting westward from the keep-tower, with sash windows. It contained the dining room, which had (according to the 1930 sale catalogue) early 18th century panelling, and the Great Hall or saloon, a two-storey

(1) Samuel Buck, 'The South Prospect of Hornby Castle The Seat of ... the Earl of Holderness'. (British Library, Landsdowne mss.912)

(2) Hornby Castle from the south-east (J. P. Neale Views of Seats, 2nd series, vol.1 (1824).)

room with a coved ceiling and bracketed cornice. This work was probably done in the time of the 3rd Earl of Holderness (d.1722).

The rest of the Castle was reconstructed for Robert Darcy, 4th Earl, who succeeded at the age of three. He was an ambassador, politician, and dilettante, and employed at least three architects — Giacomo Leoni, James Stuart and John Carr — at his numerous residences. If Stuart was employed at Hornby, it was probably in the 1750's, and it has been suggested that the fireplace, doorcases and some furnishings of the Great Hall were his. Holdernesse's main rebuilding was in the 1760's. John Carr remodelled the east and south ranges in Gothick style, with battlements, hoodmoulds to the windows, and ogee-headed glazing bars. The east range contained the private apartments, and the south range had a library and billiard room on the ground floor, and a drawing room above.

Holdernesse died in 1778, and Hornby passed to his daughter, Amelia, who married the 5th Duke of Leeds. Hornby remained in the hands of the Dukes of Leeds until 1930. Ignatius Bonomi of Durham is said to have done extensive work for the 6th Duke (d.1838), but an estimate for a riding house is the only firm evidence. There was a 19th century wing, the Bachelors' Wing, to the north of the early 18th century wing; this may have been by Bonomi.

Some furniture was sold in 1920, the Castle and its contents were sold in 1930, and most of the building was demolished.

(3) Courtyard, main entrance (C. Latham, In English Homes (1907).)

(4) Great Hall or saloon (C. Latham, In English Homes (1907).)

CLINTS HALL, Swaledale

Clints stood remarkably close to Marske Hall. The two estates followed separate descents until Clints was purchased by the Huttons of Marske in 1843, and demolished.

Samuel Buck sketched Clints in 1720, when it belonged to Charles Bathurst. It was a small, three-bay house, the centre bay projecting to form a porch. The battlements and mullioned and transomed windows suggest a 16th or 17th century building. To the left of the door, however, the old window had been replaced by two sashes.

In 1761 Charles Turner of Kirkleatham bought Clints from the Bathurst representatives, one of whom was his father, Sir William Turner. He had already been living at Clints for some years. A keen sportsman, he established a racing stables, and employed John Carr of York to make alterations in 1761. It is not clear whether the Venetian windows seen in Angus's view of 1787 were part of this scheme. The house was rough-cast in plaster at this time.

Turner sold Clints to Viscount Downe in 1767, and Downe sold it to Miles Stapleton of Drax in 1768. In 1800 the Stapleton trustees sold it to Thomas Errington of London. He lived at Clints and made many improvements to the estate. His son Michael sold Clints to Timothy Hutton of Marske in 1842. He demolished the Hall. Some outbuildings remain.

(1) Samuel Buck 'The West Prospect of Clince Hall belonging to Cha. Bathurst esq.' (British Library Landsdowne mss.914)

(2) 'Clints in Yorkshire, the Seat of Miles Stapleton Esqr.' (W. Angus, Seats of the Nobility and Gentry, 1787)

THE GREEN, Richmond

The Green, demolished 1824, was the home of the Yorkes from 1659. John Yorke built the mansion shown in Buck's 'Prospect'. It was a long, plain, late 17th century building. In the servants' hall was an early 16th century wooden carving of 'the mouth of Hell'. The extensive gardens had avenues, alleys, a mound, a summer house and the Culloden Tower (1746) by Daniel Garrett, commemorating the Jacobite defeat. Later the grounds were landscaped, and Temple Lodge was built (1769) as a menagerie. John Yorke (d.1813) was the last Yorke to occupy the Green. His nephew sold it in 1823 to repay debts.

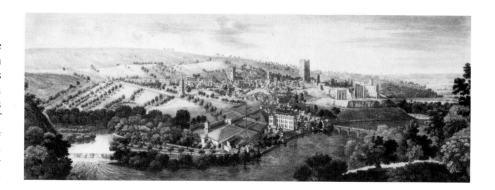

Samuel & Nathaniel Buck, 'The south west prospect of Richmond in the County of Yorke', 1749. (RCHM England)

ASKRIGG OLD HALL
Wensleydale

The Hall in the centre of Askrigg was burnt down in 1935. William Thornton built it in 1678, placing a Latin inscription over a door, with the Biblical text 'Every house is builded by some man; but he that built all things is God.' It was designed to be divided into two houses. The design was conservative: mullioned and transomed windows with arched lights, and stepped hoodmoulds over the lower doors and gable windows. The upper doors, linked by a balcony, had classical segmental pediments. The house passed to the Lightfoots: W. Lightfoot Bankes owned it in 1890; Mrs. Bankes in 1914.

Old Hall, Askrigg (Victoria County History)

HUTTON BONVILLE HALL

Hutton Bonville Hall, seat of the Peirse family in the 18th century and the Hildyards in the 19th century, was situated north of Northallerton, in a park of 90 acres stretching down to the little River Wiske. The church of St. Lawrence was adjacent, but the village had disappeared; and the setting was secluded, except for the main east-coast railway line, which passed close by.

The earliest view of the Hall is Samuel Buck's sketch, c.1720. Richard Peirse of Bedale held the Hall and manor in 1699, but by 1720 it had passed to his second son, Thomas. Buck's sketch shows Hutton Bonville in an interesting transitional state. The old Hall, 17th century (if not older) had a centre and two projecting wings, with cross-windows and gables. In 1720 one of the wings remained, but the rest of the Hall had been remodelled and refaced in ashlar in a plain 18th century style. Sash windows and flat parapets were introduced, and the centre was given a balustrade. A little later, the naive painting of the 'Hutton Bonville dog' shows the remodelling complete, and balustrades on all the parapets. The architect of the remodelling is not known.

A later 18th century view shows the Hall with pitched roofs and long, rambling wings at the back. Some of the windows at the back are old-fashioned cross-windows. The date of these alterations is not known. About 1785 Thomas Peirse's grandson, Richard William Peirse,

(1) Samuel Buck, 'The South Prospect of Hutton Bonvile The Seat of Tho. Peirse Esqr.' (British Library, Lansdowne mss.914)

(2) 'The Hutton Bonville dog', c.1725 (M. F. T. Hildyard)

sold Hutton Bonville to Anthony Hammond of Richmond. Hammond re-sold it in 1820 to Henry Peirse, M.P. for Northallerton, who had estates at nearby Lazenby. He died in 1824, and the estate passed to his daughter, Harriet, who married Sir John P. Beresford, Bart.

At some stage in the early 19th century — probably in the 1820's or early 1830's — the front of Hutton Bonville was Gothicised and given castellations. The cross-windows returned, and the centre was brought forward to form a porch and squat tower, crowned by heavy octagonal corner turrets. The architect is unknown (but the turrets resemble those of Redcar church, 1823-9, by Ignatius Bonomi of Durham).

John Richard Westgarth Hildyard bought Hutton Bonville from the Beresford-Peirse family in 1859. There were considerable additions of servants' quarters, in brick, by W. Eden Nesfield, in 1879-80. In the 1890's John Arundell Hildyard was the owner, but by 1920 had moved to Horsley Hall in County Durham. In 1921 a syndicate bought the Hutton Bonville estate and sold the farms to the tenants. The Hall, now empty, passed through a succession of owners, and Eden Nesfield's wings were demolished. The remaining part of the Hall was bought and saved by Miss V. D. Hildyard of Old Bolton Hall, Bolton-on-Swale. It passed to her sister, Cicely Hildyard, who never lived there, and she left it in 1963 to Christopher Hildyard Ringrose-Wharton of Skelton Castle. After some years of neglect, it was demolished about 1970.

(3) Late 18th century view (Lady Richmond-Brown)

(4) Hall and church (M. F. T. Hildyard)

SCRUTON HALL

Situated on the north side of the village green, near the church, Scruton Hall was the seat of the antiquary Roger Gale (c.1672-1744). Gale's father Thomas Gale (1636-1702) was Dean of York and bought the Scruton estate from Sir Abstrupus, Christopher and Anne Danby in 1688. It seems that Roger Gale built Scruton Hall about 1705. It was a modest brick building of seven bays with pediments on the front and garden sides and a tall hipped roof. According to a newspaper account of the 1953 sale, the drawing room had "charming mural decorations of the period in which it was built" – possibly plasterwork. Scruton remained in the hands of Roger Gale's descendants until 1953. The canted bays were added (supposedly) about 1820, but they were possibly earlier. Gale's grandson Henry Gale paid the architect John Foss of Richmond for "a Marble Chimney Piece in the Dining room with Wood Work &c" and a "Statuary Marble Chimney Piece in the Drawing Room with Wood Work &c" in 1797, as well as for "Planning Superintending and Measuring" unspecified work in 1794-6. Henry Gale's daughter married Lt. Col. Foster Lechmere Coore (d.1839) in 1816. On the death of Mrs. Marion Evelyn Coore in 1953 the estate was sold, and the Hall and 96 wooded acres were bought by a firm of timber merchants. No use was found for the house, and it was demolished in 1958.

(1) Garden front (Victoria County History)

(2) Entrance front (The Northern Echo)

NEWTON HOUSE
Londonderry, Bedale

A hunting seat of the 3rd Earl of Darlington (1766-1848), who was created Duke of Cleveland in 1833, Newton House was designed by Ignatius Bonomi of Durham and built in 1822-3. The stables and kennels are glowingly described in *Nimrod's Sporting Tours*.

Robert Hird wrote about Newton House in his rambling poem *Annals of Bedale*. The estate was formed in the late 18th century by Mr. Warcop, a clergyman, who built the first Newton House. Later it was the property of Robert Russell, a market gardener, whose daughter Elizabeth married Lord Darlington in 1813. Lord and Lady Darlington landscaped and improved the grounds; Thomas Robinson was the gardener.

On 1st December 1821 a storm badly damaged the house, and a chimney stack collapsed into a bedroom where a Miss Russell died of shock. The house was demolished and replaced by Bonomi's building. It was plain, probably of stuccoed brick, and had a heavy parapet and a Doric portico. To one side stretched a long wing, with a thin corner turret providing a weak picturesque effect. This wing may have been an addition for the Duchess of Cleveland (d.1866) by Lewis Vulliamy, who is recorded as working at Newton House in 1846.

The Duchess left the house to her great nephew Robert Russell. In 1914 it was the residence of William Derby Russell. The grounds became part of R.A.F. Leeming in the 1939-45 War, and Newton House was demolished in 1956.

(1) North front (Miss H. Meysey-Thompson)

(2) South front (Miss H. Meysey-Thompson)

COWESBY HALL

George Lloyd, the builder, claimed descent from the Lloyds of Llanynys of Denbigh. His cousin George lived at Stockton Hall near York and the family is also associated with Sewerby Hall in East Yorkshire.

Thomas Alston was Lord of the Manor in 1825 but by 1832 Lloyd had bought the estate and started work on the house, which stood in a sheltered horseshoe valley. He entrusted the design to Anthony Salvin, a local favourite who also worked at Sand Hutton [q.v.] and Moreby. There is a suggestion that an unidentified sketch by Salvin was a rejected design for Cowesby; what is certain is that the house as executed, with its many gables and battlemented tower, was much admired locally.

George Lloyd died in 1844, leaving Cowesby to his eldest son Thomas, and on his death it passed to his nephew William. By William's time the house had become somewhat unwelcoming and one early 20th century visitor described it as dark, damp and cold. Furthermore, guests were cured like herrings in wood smoke, as the chimneys had a propensity to blow back.

All was changed with the installation of central heating following its sale, in 1921, to Mr. Norman Adams. On the sporting front, his twelve-year-old daughter Ena ran her own pack of harriers. The house was sold again in 1926 and a subsequent owner pulled the house down, replacing it in 1949 with a more modest mock-Tudor house. The stables remain.

(1) Anthony Salvin, design (R.I.B.A. Drawings Collection)

(2) Entrance Front (Victoria County History)

UPSALL CASTLE

Dr. John Turton, Physician in Ordinary to the King, bought the Upsall estate, including the Scropes' ruined medieval castle, in 1773. Captain Edmund Turton, who succeeded to Upsall in 1857, had long cherished thoughts of a family seat on the site of the old castle, overlooking the Vale of York, near Thirsk. He built cottages, farm buildings and lodges to the design of George Goldie and even laid out gardens on the castle site before engaging Goldie & Child to design the mansion.

Their proposals, published and illustrated in *The Builder* in 1873 were for a large gothic house built of locally quarried sandstone with ashlar dressings. Dominating the design was a four-storey tower with a tall chateau-style roof, while a more modest circular turret guarded the principal entrance.

Work on the house had begun in 1872, but the house as built incorporated a number of changes imposed by the Turton family. Notable among these were the lowering of the tower and its embattlement as well as the omission of a large conservatory on the south western corner.

One Sunday morning in 1918, while Sir Edmund Turton was preaching in church, the house caught fire. A series of misfortunes culminated in the Thirsk fire brigade being unable to catch the horse that pulled the tender. By the time they arrived, all was lost. It lay in ruins until 1924, when it was rebuilt on a more modest scale, incorporating a number of fittings from nearby Wood End [q.v.].

(1) Goldie & Child's design
(The Builder 1873)

(2) View from the South West
(Lord Tranmire)

THIRKLEBY PARK, Thirsk

Thirkleby Hall was designed for Sir Thomas Frankland by James Wyatt (1746-1813) in about 1785. Wyatt's only house in the North Riding was a solid and somewhat staid block of ashlar, built on a slightly elevated site north-west of the village. From Wyatt's imposing pedimented western gateway, which survives, the Hall was approached, in Gill's words, "through a magnificent ancient avenue of Scotch Firs, considered one of the finest in this part of the kingdom."

This avenue led to the old Hall, close to the Church, which was "one of those quaint gabled houses on a rather large scale", and was probably late 16th or early 17th century. No illustration of it is known. It was entirely removed when Wyatt's new Hall was built. There had, apparently, been plans to replace it earlier: the sale catalogue of the architect Nicholas Hawksmoor mentioned eighteen plans for Thirkleby, c.1704, and designs for stables have survived.

Wyatt's house had a broad bow on the south front, flanked by tripartite windows with fan devices in the blank arches over them; and on the west front a slightly projecting triumphal arch motif, with a giant engaged Corinthian order and arched openings to either side. The entrance was on the north side, through a columned porch. The rendered wing shown on the right of the photograph was perhaps a later addition. At the back of the house was the stable·court (this survives), its archway crowned by an

(1) Thirkleby Park, east front (Sir Philip Frankland-Payne Gallwey, Bart.)

(2) View from the south-west (Sir Philip Frankland-Payne Gallwey, Bart.)

open, two-stage tower.

A good photographic record exists of many of the rooms before they were stripped prior to the 1927 demolition. Most were surprisingly plain, perhaps with a decorative cornice. One room was an octagon. The drawing room, exceptionally, had a plaster ceiling in addition to a cornice, but the rather weak banding and twisted strings of foliage were certainly not Wyatt at his most inventive. The most impressive space was the stair-hall, with its imperial staircase rising in one flight and returning in two. The ceiling was coved and top-lit, and on the landing was a screen of coupled Corinthian columns. The gravity of the composition was undoubtedly enlivened by the happy positioning of the statues of priestesses bearing votive bowls, at the foot of the stairs, though this was presumably not part of Wyatt's design.

The Franklands owned Thirkleby from 1576. Sir Thomas Frankland held the estate from 1784 to 1831 and was presumably responsible for the rebuilding, rather than his father, Admiral Sir Thomas Frankland, who held it for only a year, in 1783-4. Sir Thomas's son, Sir Robert, became Frankland-Russell in 1837 on inheriting Chequers Court, Buckinghamshire. He left Thirkleby to his widow, Lady Frankland Russell, in 1849, and it passed to her daughter Emily, who married Sir William Payne-Gallwey. She assumed the name Payne-Frankland in 1882 and died in 1913. The family sold Thirkleby shortly before its demolition in 1927.

(3) Staircase hall (Sir Philip Frankland-Payne Gallwey, Bart.)

(4) Drawing room (Sir Philip Frankland-Payne Gallwey, Bart.)

WOOD END,
Thornton-le-Street

Wood End is just one name for this house, which stood to the west of Thornton-le-Street, near Thirsk. Jeffrey's map of Yorkshire (surveyed 1767-70) describes it as Woodhall — it then became Wood End and latterly Thornton-le-Street Hall. Local people always refer to it as Gaultby.

John Talbot settled at the Old Hall, north of the village, in 1549. The first reference to a house on the site of Wood End was in 1637 but it was many years before the head of the family made the move from the Old Hall.

Roger, the last of the Talbot line died in 1778 but not before he had done major works at Wood End. The plasterwork was finely executed and was of c.1760. Later descriptions of the house dwell on the first floor picture gallery, 120 feet long, suggesting that Roger's alterations incorporated an earlier building of the late sixteenth or early seventeenth century. The architect is not known but the house was the subject of "considerable additions" after the Talbot heirs sold the estate in 1793.

The new owner was Samuel Crompton of Derby. The Cromptons were an eminent family of bankers; both Samuel and his father had twice been mayors of the city. Crompton's alterations were carried out in about 1800 and an engraving dated 1822 shows a handsome south front of nine bays, the centre delicately defined by four pilasters below a frieze, itself capped by a large pediment

(1) South front 1822 by Jones (York Minster Library)

(2) View from the South West (Earl Cathcart)

with cartouche and surmounted by three urns. Just to the west is a pretty gothic summer house which may have led to one of the grottoes adorning the grounds.

Samuel Crompton was succeeded by his son, also Samuel, created a baronet in 1838. When Sir Samuel died in 1848 his eldest daughter and co-heiress, Elizabeth Mary inherited. In 1850 she married Lord Greenock, who succeeded his father as the 3rd Earl Cathcart in 1859. In about 1884 the house was again altered; contemporary reports talk of it being almost entirely remodelled. The result cannot be judged a great success. The house was clad in stone, which submerged the pleasing pilasters to the south front. Although the main pediment survived, its junior partner over the front door was replaced by a balustraded balcony. Further balustrading round the roof necessitated the removal of the stone urns seen in the earlier print and an Italianate tower appeared to the rear.

Elizabeth's son, the 4th Earl, succeeded in 1905. Following his death in 1911 the house was let. In about 1921 the house was sold to a consortium of local farmers, timber merchants and antique dealers known as the forty thieves. They dismantled it, leaving the 18th century stables and a pair of lodges which have been described as the most perfect classical boxes in Britain.

(3) Drawing Room (Earl Cathcart)

(4) Dining Room (Earl Cathcart)

SION HILL

The three-storey central block was late eighteenth century and although the name of the builder is not known, by 1812 it was described as the seat of the late Edward D'Oyley Esq.

By 1828 it was the seat of Joshua Crompton, whose brother Samuel owned the adjoining Wood End estate [q.v.]. He was probably responsible for adding the two large wings. In 1867 it was bought by the Hon. George Lascelles. His executors sold to Percy Stancliffe in 1911. The following year the house was demolished and replaced by a worthy successor to the designs of Walter Brierley.

Sion Hill (H. W. Mawer Museum Trust)

HOLBECK HALL
Scarborough

An undistinguished mock-Tudor house designed by John Sedding and built as a private residence in 1883, just to the south of Scarborough.

The dramatic departure of Holbeck Hall over the cliff edge in 1993 made it, for a time, perhaps the world's most celebrated lost house.

The rose garden disappeared before breakfast one summer morning and within days most of the rest of the house had followed. It became the resort's major tourist attraction and must be the only lost house to have had its demise marked by the production of specially made souvenir T-shirts.

Holbeck Hall 1993 (Yorkshire Evening Press)

YORK

The boundaries of York have been taken as they stood in 1973, before local government re-organisation.

In the following pages there are illustrations of a number of York houses which have been lost, most of them this century. They represent only a proportion of those that have gone and it is ironic that although seen on a regular basis by far more people than their country cousins, the city's houses were generally not as well recorded. Several houses for which no illustrative material has been found are none the less worthy of mention:-

Nunthorpe Hall – demolition 1977 (D. Buttery)

GROVE LODGE Almost certainly the house that Mr. Bellerby, a bookseller from Stonegate, built on Haxby Road circa 1832, using materials from the Old Deanery [q.v.], which it was said to resemble. Later, Henry Newton, solicitor, lived there. Demolished about 1900, for redevelopment.

GROVE HOUSE An early 19th century house off Huntington Road probably built by Robert "Dobbin" Cattle, a jeweller and mail coach proprietor who died there in 1842. It was eventually surrounded by terraced housing and demolished in the early years of this century.

HEWORTH PLACE Later known as The Pleasaunce. There was a house on the site, bounded by Heworth Road and Stockton Lane, in 1843. Initially a private house, it spent its later years as an asylum. Demolished in the 1930's.

OLD MANOR HOUSE, HEWORTH A modest farmhouse with late 18th century additions which stood on the south side of the village street. Demolished between the wars.

FULFORD LODGE An early 19th century house lived in by Miss Cholmley but renamed Kilburn House by Joseph Agar, York tanner, after he bought it in the 1870's. Demolished between the wars. Kilburn Road was built on the site.

FULFORD FIELD HOUSE A large house built before 1843 in elaborate gardens near Fulford Cross. By 1861 it was Mrs. Armstrong's Ladies' School and remained in educational use into this century. A modern school now occupies the site. The lodge remains.

OLD NUNTHORPE A large house formed from a pair of early 19th century villas on the east side of Bishopthorpe Road. From the late 19th century to his death in 1939, it was the seat of Sir Wilfred Thomson, Bt. Demolished 1950's.

DRINGHOUSES MANOR F. W. Shepherd reclad Col. Eason Wilkinson's earlier house after buying the estate in the 1940's. His family sold most of the site to Trust House Hotels, who demolished it in 1966 but retained the large cedar in the grounds.

HOLGATE VILLA A large house of circa 1840 standing in Holgate Road, built by the York & North Midland Railway as a company house for their engineers. It was replaced by an office block in the 1960's.

WEST BANK Built in 1853 by James Backhouse Jnr., overlooking his nursery in Acomb. A plain Victorian house with a centre flanked by gabled wings. Bought by Sir James Hamilton in 1910 and later a home for unmarried mothers. Demolished 1974/5. A church occupies the site.

ACOMB PRIORY Acomb Priory only acquired this misnomer in the late 19th century. In the 1840's it was simply Plantation Hall. It lay in a small park off Boroughbridge Road. Still there in 1932, it was subsequently replaced by a printing works and housing.

OUSECLIFFE Built in the 1850's for William Hudson, an ecclesiastical lawyer, to the designs of J. B. & W. Atkinson. White brick with a large tower, overlooking the Ouse at Clifton. Bought by the army in 1907 as headquarters of Northern Command and renamed Government House. Demolished 1965.

BURTON GRANGE Built for the Wallis family, York bankers, circa 1840 on the north side of Burton Stone Lane. A modest villa, it was later a girls' school. Demolished for housing development in the 1930's.

BELLE VUE HOUSE

Belle Vue House stood on rising ground off Heslington Road.

William Abbey Plows bought the site in 1833 and probably had the house built shortly after that date. He chose the gothic style, which was unusual for York, and supplied the carved stone decorations from his own workshops in Walmgate.

A fairly modest two-storey three-bay central block in white brick was enlivened by Plows' ogee stonework. The same pattern was repeated in the castellated turrets which flanked the central block. Surmounting the whole was the lantern — a viewing platform with stairs from the landing. The whole composition made it York's most distinctive 19th century villa.

Outside, Plows decorated the garden with various ornaments and, curiously, three carved stone capitals from Carlton House, the palace designed by Henry Holland for the Prince of Wales, demolished in 1826.

Plows tried selling the house in 1846 and the particulars reveal such luxuries as soft water supplied to the dressing rooms, a water closet and a bathroom. He eventually achieved a sale in 1852. Subsequent owners included Charles Etty, a sugar fabricant who named it, temporarily, Java Hall.

Its days as a private house ended in 1879 when it was acquired by The Retreat for use as a nurses home. In 1935 all but the ground floor shell was demolished. What was left acted as a screen to a swimming pool but this fell into disuse and the site was cleared in 1985/6.

(1) View from the South-East (The Retreat)

(2) View from the South (The Retreat)

NORTH LODGE

An early 19th century villa which was built by the York and North Midland Railway in Bishopfields, just outside the city walls. It had the unusual distinction of being demolished circa 1873 to make way for the world's largest railway station.

The house had been let rent free to John Close, when he was the secretary to the railway during the reign of George Hudson. Close was later a woollen draper, iron founder and wine merchant. Increasing congestion at the old station made it imperative for the then North Eastern Railway to construct a new station outside the walls. Close's house stood in the way. Although prepared to move, he refused to accept cash as compensation and instead insisted that the company build him a new house, The Hollies, now known as the Chase Hotel, on Tadcaster Road.

North Lodge circa 1870 (Evelyn Collection)

DUKE'S HALL

Edmund Barker's Prospect of York (1718) shows a large house, prominently placed above the city on Bishophill. This was Duke's Hall, the Duke of Buckingham's house of circa 1620 which was said to have been the grandest house in York. Similar in style and date to the Treasurer's House but on a far larger scale, it presented nine bays on its principal fronts, under large shaped gables. A later 18th century engraving shows it in ruins. Today, Buckingham Street serves as a reminder of its presence.

Edmund Barker's Prospect of York 1718

HEWORTH HALL

With eleven bedrooms, Heworth Hall was perhaps the largest of the villas that sprang up in Heworth following the enclosure awards of the early 19th century. Built in about 1830 by Mrs. Lucy Willey, and her husband Jocelyn, curate of St. Cuthberts, it was in a conservative classical style. In 1859 Lady Milbanke lived there, then in the closing years of the century, Thomas Brogden.

In 1928 the house and twelve acres of grounds, described as a "valuable building estate" were sold by auction. Semi-detached houses advanced up the drive and the house was demolished in 1934.

Heworth Hall 1934 (H. Gibbs)

GLEN HEWORTH

Glen Heworth, later simply known as The Glen, is shown on the 1850 Ordnance Survey Map down Bull Lane, south of East Parade. Miss Lawson lived there in 1857. William Leak, a draper and founder of York's best known department store had moved there by 1867. He doubled the size of the house and filled spare bedrooms by letting them to his shop assistants.

The grounds were whittled away over the years, to create both public gardens and private housing. Dr. Lythe lived there between the wars but it was pulled down by York Corporation circa 1965.

Glen Heworth (M. Lythe)

TANG HALL

Tang Hall was first mentioned in the 13th century. However, it was James Barber's house of circa 1830 that elevated it to the status of a gentleman's villa. Typical of York, it had deep overhanging eaves, suggesting the Atkinsons as architects. Barber, a silversmith and coach proprietor in Coney Street, sold the house to Captain Starkey. Starkey died in 1906 but his widow Lady Evelyne lived there into increasingly eccentric old age, shooting trespassers with grapeshot.

On her death in 1925 York Corporation bought the estate and developed it for housing, although the house survived for some time as a pub.

Tang Hall (D. Wilde)

HEWORTH COTTAGE

This was some cottage. The 17th century house was probably the one that appears on the Hearth Tax as occupied by John Kilvington. The Kilvington heirs sold in 1736 and it passed through the hands of the Johnson family before being sold to Thomas Bond, stage coach proprietor. His daughter Ann inherited.

Ann left the property to Lucy Moore, a comparative stranger who shared her religious views and she it was who built the later Heworth Hall [q.v.] in the grounds. The last owners were the Bartons. It disappeared about 1937.

Heworth Cottage 1937 (J. Kaner)

HOLGATE LODGE

Thomas Simpson, a Knaresborough doctor, bought land in Holgate in 1827 and by 1832 had built what was initially called Holgate Villa. A lodge on Poppleton Road led through parkland to a rather severe, squat house.

Following Simpson's death in 1863, it was sold to John Gutch, a lawyer. He and his wife Eliza moved in in 1868 and together they built up a small estate which eventually included Holgate Windmill. Eliza died in 1931, fifty years after her husband and stipulated in her will that the house was to be demolished and the grounds sold for building.

Holgate Lodge – view from the South (D. Lodge)

NUNTHORPE HALL

This was one of the most lavish of York's Victorian houses, with a sumptuous interior looking out over the Knavesmire. It became one of the great centres of York's social life when Sir Edward Green moved there in 1888, although the style suggests a slightly earlier house.

During the First World War Ethel Lycett Green ran the house as a military hospital but by 1921 it had passed out of the family's hands. For many years it survived as flats in the ownership of John Hetherton, whose family sold it for development. It was demolished in 1977 and replaced by flats.

Nunthorpe Hall – 19th century engraving (P. Hyde)

THE GOVERNOR'S HOUSE, York Castle

The Governor of York Prison lived in what was probably the only circular house in the city. It stood in the grounds of Samuel Ward's house, which was bought and demolished to enable improvements to be carried out to the prison in the 1830's. The architects of the three-storey battlemented building were P. F. Robinson and G. T. Andrews. It was completed in about 1835.

The civil prison closed in 1900 and the complex assumed a military role until 1929. After lying disused for five years, the buildings were bought by the City and demolished in 1935.

The Governor's House 1852 by William Pumphrey
(H. Murray)

MIDDLETHORPE LODGE

An early nineteenth century white brick house typical of the villas built to the south west of York, in this instance on Tadcaster Road. The site is marked by Middlethorpe Drive and Middlethorpe Grove.

It is best remembered as the home of Sir John Grant Lawson M.P., one time Deputy Speaker of the House of Commons.

Its most striking feature was the later four-storey observation tower in the Arts and Crafts style.

It was requisitioned in 1941 and remained in Army use until its demolition in 1953/4.

Garden Front 1966 (Sir Peter Shepherd)

THE OLD DEANERY (1)

This ancient building stood to the south of the Minster on the site now occupied by the Minster School. In 1640 Charles I convened a Great Council of the Realm which met in The Deanery, whose hall was hung with tapestry for the occasion.

Long before the creation of Deangate, carriages came and went through a side passage which led into Petergate.

When it was demolished in 1831 and replaced by a new house [q.v.] the materials were bought by Mr. Bellerby, a bookseller in Stonegate, who built a new house on Haxby Road "quite resembling the original".

The Old Deanery (1) Sketch by W. Monkhouse (York Minster Library)

THE OLD DEANERY (2)

The 19th century Deanery stood on the north side of the Minster and was completed in 1831 to the designs of J. P. Pritchett at a cost of £8000. The foundations had been laid in 1827 but work was held up for twelve months due to the 1829 Minster fire.

Hargrave's guide to York (1838) concluded that it would "stand through the ages as a memorial to the spirited and refined taste of Dean Cockburn". In fact, it lasted little over 100 years and was demolished in 1937 following the completion of its neo-Georgian successor.

The Old Deanery (2) (York Minster Library)

INDEX

Grid ref.   Page

YORK

BIBLIOGRAPHY

H. B. Browne, *Chapters of Whitby history 1823-1946. The story of the Whitby Literary and Philosophical Society and of Whitby Museum*, 1946.

Samuel Buck's Yorkshire sketchbook, Wakefield Historical Publications, 1980

T. Bulmer and Co., *History, topography and directory of North Yorkshire*, 1890

Darrell Buttery, *The vanished buildings of York*, n.d.

[John Carr]. *The works in architecture of John Carr*, York Georgian Society, 1973.

Christopher Clarkson, *The history of Richmond*, 1821.

H. M. Colvin, *A biographical dictionary of British architects, 1660-1840,* 1978.

Anne Ashley Cooper, *Yorke country*, 1989

Country Life magazine:
'Stanwick Park, Yorkshire, the seat of Eleanor, Duchess of Northumberland', 17 February 1900.
'Hornby Castle, Yorkshire, the seat of the Duke of Leeds', 14 July 1906.
Lawrence Weaver, 'Rounton Grange, Yorkshire a seat of Sir Hugh Bell, Bart.', 26 June 1915.
Christopher Hussey, 'Halnaby Hall, Yorkshire', 1-8 April 1933.
John Cornforth, 'Kirkleatham, Cleveland', 6, 20 January 1977.
Giles Worsley, 'Hornby Castle, Yorkshire the home of Mr. Roger Clutterbuck', 29 June 1989.

Rosemary Curry, Sheila Kirk, *Philip Webb in the North*, (exhibition catalogue, Teeside branch, RIBA), 1984.

Thomas Gill, *Vallis Eboracensis*, 1852.

William Grange, *The Vale of Mowbray*, 1859

John Graves, *History of Cleveland,* 1808

John Harris and Gervase Jackson-Stops (ed.), *Britannia illustrata. Knyff and Kip,* 1984.

B. J. D. Harrison, Grace Dixon (ed.) *Guisborough before 1900,* 1982.

Jane Hatcher, *Richmondshire architecture,* 1990.

Robert Hird, *Annals of Bedale,* ed. Lesley Lewis, North Yorks., County Record Office, 1975.

Michael Holmes, *The country house described. An index to the country houses of Great Britain,* 1986.

W. G. M. Jones Barker, *Historical and topographical account of Wensleydale,* 1856.

North Riding Record Office. Annual Report, 1971, 'The Zetland (Dundas) archive'.

John W. Ord, *The history and antiquities of Cleveland,* 1846.

N. Pevsner, *The Buildings of England, Yorkshire: the North Riding*, 1966.

N. Pevsner *The Buildings of England, Yorkshire: York and the East Riding*, 1972

B. N. Reckitt, *A history of the Sir Philip Reckitt Educational Trust*, 1988.

RCHM England, *Houses of the North York Moors,* 1987.

John Rushton, *The Ryedale Story,* a *Yorkshire countryside handbook*, n.d.

SAVE Britain's heritage, *Vanishing houses of England*, 1982.

William H. Scott, *The North and East Ridings at the opening of the 20th century: contemporary biographies*, (W. T. Pike, ed.), 1903.

Anna Sproule, *Lost Houses of Britain,* 1981.

H. E. C. Stapleton, G. G. Pace, J. E. Day, *A skilful master builder. The continuing story of a Yorkshire family business. Craftsmen for seven generations,* 1975.

Roy Strong, Marcus Binney, John Harris, *The destruction of the country house,* 1974.

Victoria County History. Yorkshire, North Riding, 1914-23.

John Warburton, 'Journal in 1718-19 of John Warburton..', *Yorkshire Archaeological Journal,* 15, (1900).

T. Whellan and Co., *History and topography of the City of York and the North Riding of Yorkshire*, 1857-9.

T. D. Whitaker, *An history of Richmondshire*, 1823.

William White, *History, gazetteer and directory of the East and North Ridings of Yorkshire*, 1840.